They'll Be Good for Seed

They'll Be Good for Seed

Contemporary Hungarian Poetry

Translated by
Gabor G. Gyukics & Michael Castro

WHITE PINE PRESS / BUFFALO, NEW YORK

White Pine Press
P.O. Box 236
Buffalo, NY 14201
www.whitepine.org

Publication of this book was made possible, in part, with support from The Witter Bynner Foundation for Poetry and within the framework of cooperation according to the objectives of the Petőfi Literary Fund (www.plf.hu) promoting Hungarian literature.

PETŐFI LITERARY FUND

Printed and bound in the United States of America.

Cover Image: "Fractals" by Julia Lunk. Watercolor, 2009. Used by permission of the artist. www.lunkjuliworks.blogspot.com

ISBN: 978-1-945680-49-6

Library of Congress number: 2020952142

Acknowledgments

"1990" and "The Visit" by Dénes Krusovszky, "Bauxite" by Marió Z. Nemes, "Caravaggio" by Gábor Lanczkor, "Two Kinds of Dark" by János Térey, "that boy" by Zita Murányi, and "report poem" by Zsuka Nagy were all originally published in *Panel* magazine.

"Byron Burns Shelley's Corpse on the Shore" by Gabor Lanczkor appeared in *North Dakota Quarterly.*

"Triangle" by Júlia Lázár appeared in *American and Others* anthology, Italy.

"Announcement" by János Térey was first published in *A Fine Line: New Poetry from Eastern and Central Europe*, Arc Publications, Todmorden, England, 2004.

"Evening Milk" by Márió Z. Nemes.; "m2" by Zsuka Nagy; "Before New Moon," "Eyes Blossoming," and "Flood" by János Áfra; and "Cold and Denial" by Mónika Mesterházi appeared in *Unlikely Stories.*

"Immortality" and "Two in the Street" by Zsuka Nagy *Anomaly* magazine.

"Mist" by Szabina Ughy appeared in *Poet Lore.*

"Lover's Dream," "Blind Map," and "Talking" by Krisztina Tóth appeared in *New Poetry in Translation.*

"The Source" by Dénes Krusovszky appeared in *Arkansas International.*

"Hawk, Reverse and Ice" by Anna T. Szabó appeared in *The Blue Nib Literary Magazine.*

"blooming and decomposing…," "step into the together-time of objects…," "the globe made of glass…," and "until I don't place myself…" by Johanna Domonkos appeared in *Sensitive Skin.*

"A Day on Earth (Interlude)" by Gabor G. Gyukics appeared in *Blue Nib* and in *American and Others* anthology, Italy.

"impossibilism," "guardian angels," "visit," and "encyclical" by Gabor G. Gyukics appeared in *Sensitive Skin.*

"lost goon stick seen at the Amalfi Coast" by Gabor G. Gyukics appeared in in *Big Bridge.*

"volumetric analysis" by Gabor G. Gyukics appeared in *From the Ancestors* anthology

Table of Contents

Translator's Preface

A new anthology of contemporary Hungarian poetry is long overdue in the United States. This anthology showcases the work of eight women and eight men between the ages of thirty-three and sixty-three and from many different backgrounds. When I was working on the biographies, I came across Zsuka Nagy's remark, "I hate biographies. Read the poems to determine who the poet is." The prizes a poet receives are incidental. How you should write and what you should read is subjective. I had an eye-opening experience at a university lecture in the U.S. The professor named several poets and admonished, "Don't ever read these poets if you want to be a good poet." My blood boiled! Let the student, the editor, and the reader peruse the world's shelves and decide what to read and how to assimilate that into his/her own writing and life.

So, don't read the biographies first. Start with the Introduction and then settle in with the poems. Start with any poem. My approach to editing is different from that of many editors: I choose the poems, not the poets.

Michael Castro, my co-translator for several decades, and I published our first anthology of Hungarian poetry, *Swimming in the Ground,* in 2003. We collaborated on the selection of poems for this anthology, and he was able to fine-tune some of the translations before becoming ill. Unfortunately, Michael passed away in the winter of 2018. A great poet and a great friend, we are lucky to have his mind-print in this anthology. For other poems, I asked a few American poet friends whom I knew and admired to step in

Most of these poems came from magazines. After I read them, I began to read more from the poets, either in books or online. Then I asked the poets whose work I found compelling to send me a selection of their work, and Michael and I selected the poems for this volume from what they sent. Often, what they chose and what I had first seen and admired were the same poems. It seemed we were on the same track.

The result is an anthology that is diverse and original. Filled with captivating subjects, musicality, rhythm, and colorful images, these are the poems that captured our attention.

—Gabor G. Gyukics

Introduction

Translated by Gabor G. Gyukics

The Temptation of the Preface

I pondered for days about how to start the preface to this anthology presenting contemporary Hungarian poetry. In truth, I postponed the task. I seemed to have an inexplicable obstacle inside me. Was that a cop out?

According to Jacques Derrida, a preface is ridiculous:

> "From the viewpoint of the foreword, which recreates the intention-to-say after the fact, the text exists as something written—a past—which under the false appearance of a present, a hidden omnipotent author (in full mastery of his product) is presenting to the reader as his future. Here is what I wrote, then read, and what I am writing that you are going to read. After which you will again be able to take possession of this preface which in sum you have not yet begun to read, even though, once having read it, you will already have anticipated everything that follows and thus might just as well dispense with reading the rest."
>
> —*Dissemination*

The preface might superfluously fuss about things and obtrude upon the choices of the reader. The ideal preface to this selection of poems, I thought, would be one that would erase itself at the moment it was read. It would become the resistance to itself. After all, resistance is one of the most important sources of poetry—the force that bursts ragged words, cliched phrases, slogans, ideologies, and kitschy bubbles apart.

It would be a lot easier for me if this anthology were created for extraterrestrials. They don't have any preconceptions about Hungarian and American literature and culture. But it looks like extraterrestrials aren't rushing out to get their hands on poetry books. They have no idea that this would be the best way to hide among us: the libraries are filled with invisible poetry aficionados. One might think poetry is dead, that only a few readers remain, and that dog-eared books by some long-dead and boring poets moulder on dusty bookshelves in suburban libraries. Suddenly a poetry book disappears from the shelf. Then another and another, and finally someone becomes curious and leafs through a book or an anthology. One can conjure a sci-fi feeling by disappearing into poetry. Like an extraterrestrial, you can escape the boundaries of your body. Switch to warp speed and you'll embarrass a spacecraft. Don't worry about the library's security guards; they won't see you floating above the stairs as you move from floor to floor. As you turn the pages of poetry books from different cultures, you'll have favorite lines that you'll remember years later, even though you don't remember the poet's name and don't speak his/her language, especially if it's the language of a nation as small as Hungary.

The universe is here. All you have to do is to reach your hand toward the poetry bookshelves. "Universe" is a simple word. Nevertheless in a poem words are not only simple. Many times when I read a good poem, it seems the silence of infinite space calls out. What is alien and frightening becomes familiar. This is precisely where I feel fellowship with my ideal extraterrestrial readers. It's the same fellowship I might feel with our future American and other English-speaking readers, despite the insurmountable differences between languages and the necessary distortions, modifications and transformations that occur in translation.

"I find it helpful to remind myself that there are worlds outside my world. Call them universes, if you like; but I am less interested in the 'uni' than the verses," says Charles Bernstein, one of the gurus of American poetry, in the preface to the first book of his selected work, published in Hungarian translation a few years ago. Translation is one way to expand poetry's universe.

It's a cliché that works live on in new forms through translation. We acknowledge that there is no perfect translation and accept that in some cases the translation is better than the original and that countless translations of a work are possible. The anthology edited by Gábor G. Gyukics, an American-Hungarian poet and translator who has lived in the United States, wasn't created to meet the canonical expectations of contemporary Hungarian literature. He trusts his own impressions and taste and hopes they will meet with the readers'. This collection includes mainstream poets who are well-known and a few who are not.

The 20th century Hungarian writer, Sándor Márai, author of *Embers*, wrote in his diary that: "There are no great poets. There are only good poems." Márai, whose work was banned in Hungary until the political changes in 1989, spent half his life as an immigrant in America, his last years in San Diego, California. Poetry was one of his everyday necessities. He didn't revere poets; he revered good poems. Gyukics' method is similar to his: he's not choosing poets; he's selecting poems. Although the subjective and text-centered procedure is somewhat colored by a framework of diversity in age and gender, the authors' biographies didn't play any role in the final selections.

Gyukics' anthology manifests an alternative literary understanding. Being alternative allows for questioning official historiography and points out the incomplete details that are walled up by canonical ideology and the cul-de-sac of elitism. Freedom of diversity permeates Gyukics' selection and his translation experiences with his American poet-friend, Michael Castro (1945-2018).

The term "anthology" is from the Greek word *anthologia*, from *anthos* "flower" and *logia*, "collection." Gyukics poetic bouquet contains carnivorous flowers that hunger for the tissue, muscle and organs of the body. There are flowers that reveal nature and landscape as freed from expectations of subjectivity and tradition. Then there are flowers whose shapes are reminiscent of a turn-of-the-century flower, but their color, feel, and scent evoke contemporary unrest. And there are flowers that can't be placed anywhere, that don't fit in any vase. How the hell did they get here? You put them on a shelf but the next day you shake your head: it doesn't look right. The shapes of some flowers are too complicated and they speak in a rambling flower language. Still you can't resist. Then there are flowers that if you smell them, you'll die. After you die, you're born again as Hungarian. Suddenly you feel you're a stranger in America and your homeland is Hungary. You enroll to a language course; with much misery you learn Hungarian and soon enough you're looking for an apartment in Budapest or in Szeged. So be careful with those poetic flowers: they aren't only flesh-eaters they're identity eaters as well.

In the past twenty years, free verse became dominant in Hungarian poetry. In the '90s, after the political change, language variations and irony played a big role, but the cult of traditionally-structured poetry was still alive. By now, it's pretty much gone. Here and there one can find traditional poetic forms, including the sonnet, which is the super form of "Le Parnasse et le Symbolisme," but it's nostalgia for an era when art existed for art although it wasn't exactly true at that time either. French and Hungarian symbolists had their own socially-engaged pieces. The turn-of-the-century "ivory tower," where the artist hid from the crowd, had cracked, and it eventually collapsed under the cultural hegemony of late capitalism.

Hungary's political crisis in the new millennium, the "Kulturkampf," that aimed for a homogeneous identity against exploitative globalization and the nationalism that paradoxically served big business, provoked a critical attitude in poetry.

At the beginning of the 21ST century, young poets of the new millennium were described as the first generation after the "end of history." A few years have passed and it turned out that history is like the Hydra of Lern. For every head chopped off, the Hydra regrew two heads. In the post-truth era of capitalism, versions of history multiplied and forms of resistance were exposed to the diluting machinery of ideology.

Then came the more direct social criticism and commitment of slam poetry, which influenced the work of traditional non-performance authors. The politicization of aesthetics, perception, and public poetry are on the agenda again, manifest in post-humanist lyricism, the hungaro-futurist movement that turns political speech inside out, and in the works of climate-conscious authors.

In Hungary, after the political upheaval, the debate about canon was ambiguous. The place of authors silenced during the dictatorship of the socialist state is still problematic in literary history. Like Hungarian society, Hungarian literature operates in the essence of division based on the image of the enemy. The rural-urban controversy continues and lives on under the pseudo name of right and left. Furthermore they are not interested in each other. Sándor Márai's remark from his 1944 war diary is still valid: "These 'rural' writers quarrel in their vanity and huffiness like old divas, and these 'urban' writers replace what's missing from their talent and character with lexical knowledge, and there's a lack of generosity of true talent everywhere…"

Nevertheless, I can disclose several positive things, as well. After the unfortunate termination of the Hungarian journal *Nagyvilág*, which published world literature and closely monitored American literature, two new online journals are publishing world literature (*versumonline.hu, 1749.hu*). More and more female authors reflect issues of female identity, and alternative gender identities are encountered more frequently in literature. Although experimental poetry is not part of the mainstream as in other European countries, it's not considered awkward, and no longer banned, as it was during the dictatorships. Before 1989, books by American authors appeared sporadically in Hungary. In the past few years several books by American poets have been published: Anne Carson, Charles Bernstein, Charles Bukowski, Billy Collins, Frank O'Hara, Ira Cohen, Jim Northrup, John Ashbery, to mention just a few. Gábor G. Gyukics, who translates in both directions, has played an important role in this. No wonder he was awarded a Lifetime Achievement Award by the National Beat Poetry Foundation in 2020.

It's important to mention that this is the second Hungarian poetry anthology edited by Castro and Gyukics. Twenty long years have passed since the first one, so it would be worth comparing the two books to get a more detailed picture of the arc of Hungarian verse. The archives of the New York Public Library holds several anthologies of Hungarian poetry in English. Gyukics' obsessive enterprise is a new piece in the jigsaw puzzle of American-Hungarian cultural relations. Michael Castro, his co-translator died in 2018, so their mutual endeavor, the publication of this book, is a celebration: the linguistic resurrection of an American poet—with the help of Hungarian poetry.

—Roland Orcsik,
poet, editor

They'll Be Good for Seed

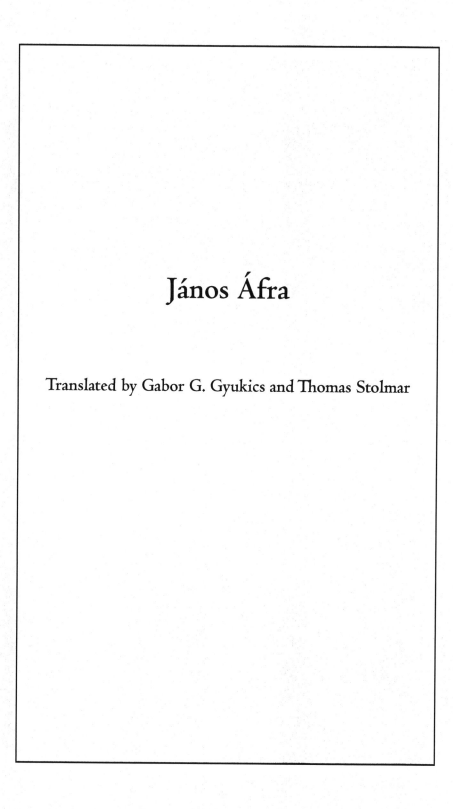

János Áfra

Translated by Gabor G. Gyukics and Thomas Stolmar

The Last Garden

It begins when dazed frogs fall
at your feet in a hailstorm, expecting you
to grow branches above them and take root
within your outstretched arms.

It begins when deep rumbles tip things over
and the ground shakes beneath your feet,
but city-sized black circles all around
remain infrangible.

It begins when the moon enshrouds the sun
and even as the finest astronomers stare
in disbelief, wagons and bodies collide
because the lamps are lit for only you.

It begins when a shrill scream
claws the eardrums, knocks down bridges
confuses birds' flight until you begin
to speak and all becomes quiet.

It begins when earth perspires from within
and new islands emerge in molten spots,
volcanoes simultaneously erupt, burying
those far away from you.

It begins when a lonely child lies silently
upon a beach before flood tide, but
you're not leaving because your heart
breaks and you sob.

This is how it begins.

Flood

Again, the morning finds you at the river
looking at your bare feet, deciding
to glide through the new day,
whatever may happen to the distant dead.
You're ticking on, crackling with visibility
the way light rises, climbing on the stones
of the road; a clocktower follows
the awakening horizon, yet bones
sleep in the shade of the western wall.
Smoldering color returns to a the awakened sky
as you bend to water filled with snakes.
Reencountering yourself between
your palms, submerging your disavowed
face into your human face,
you strain yesterday's emotions through
the web of your fingers.
You freed the pigeon who died that morning,
exhausted from flight,
an unfathomable message from thousands
of miles away tied to its leg
The bell clanged
the previous dusk above you.
Certainly, you could not heal the broken skull
which fell at your feet with jerking
wings, yet you made death a little easier.
Cranial cracks, muscles no longer moving,
yet this pigeon was a foreign gray god
as you colored the early morning river
red with its blood.

After Someone

Carry yourself in a thousand directions,
break the unbreakable unity
scattered all over, betraying nothing.
Your left-behind traces scintillate in endless
spaces and from a distance your fragments
might recognize each other.
Let sky be a coterie of apathy
where invisible entities await,
let the world ring with emotions
where bodies are created & decomposed,
permitting time for lines of possibility
to invoke your thousand faces branching off
through these motions.
Cultivate desire, instinct & fear,
disallow anyone to see through this life
disguised as whimsical... Let them coalesce
freely, but don't allow your open wounds
to rule their coiling fates
lest their every decision feed
what's imperishable in you.
This will which builds connections shall become
the privilege of but a few who heal, who
though distorting, begin repeating relevant
sentences, converting your hidden shapes.

Before New Moon

Open your window,
throw out the ennui
which consumes itself
through the depths of your house
the center of your chest
slowly making
memories pervious...
Cut it out completely,
give room to those
still with you.
Give room to the facts
that surround you,
slowly constricting your
perforated existence.
Let your ancient pain
rise to the surface
let your wrinkled
face shatter.
Let the sound
rip through you.

Eyes Blossoming

If your decision won't let you rest
enter the hall of attention,
turn the portraits inward. Your
fragile bonds with your ancestors
will hold you together.
Ask as you await the inevitable
fall, eyes separate from you by time,
bloom on the tender wall
and enter you... From the leaking
abyss of perception mist spreads,
gets beneath your skin,
and you fall from vision
to vision, a blossoming then
withering of nocturnal pupils'
circling inside you. Already past
pictures enough for decades,
crushed & crumbled in seconds,
dissolved, as you reach
another point of levitation
and faint into luminous
silence.

Silent Stones

Chase your affliction
from head to neck,
from neck to shoulders,
from shoulders to chest,
from chest to guts,
from guts to ass,
from ass to legs,
from legs to feet,
and the world will
swallow it all.

Undeciphered Message

The reason for your sore throat
could be an anxiety tracing
back to an old buried object.
For example, if, while gardening,
you come upon an old chain
which at daybreak
turns around your neck,
then at a crossroads, say, "Shoo!
Shoo! Shoo!"
With this your angina will
go away! Then leave
the chain on the spot.

The Leader

Go to the fire ring
where, before leaving,
spirits breathe freely.
Make a fire in front of the hut,
throw in myrrh branches
to soothe the relatives' pain.
Smoke spreading
over the city helps dissolve
bonds with the deceased.
Though the door's open,
they won't flee.
Stand upon the threshold
and burn incense, which keeps
them velveted in time
before their passage,
after the stressful recognition
that inevitably catches you, too,
Remove your shoes,
bravely face the home
of dust that is your body.
Roll rice dumplings
boiled in milky water
amid the fire's ashes
and murmur the sentences
of the attendant helpers.
Place the kneaded objects
in your mouth and swallow
to your very soul.
Already inviolable, this warrior
has dropped in on you
to be an apprentice
you can now trust
to lead your fucked-up life.

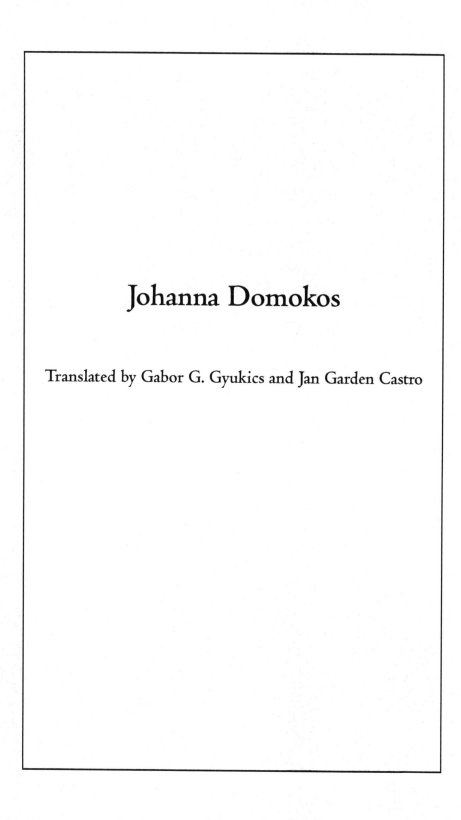

Johanna Domokos

Translated by Gabor G. Gyukics and Jan Garden Castro

blooming and decomposing moments absorb inside me,
touch, and my face shares in everything blooming decomposing,
absorbing inside me to recognize why I came to the intersecting lines
of something to make me believe
pain can turn to joy
what makes a difference inside my body
now when the river must be crossed
now when the blood must be crossed

waiting for the news to cry
from over here: go over there, everything is easier
she who cries cries beautifully loves everyone
you watch me and laugh
as I fallllllllllll into the pit you dug

if the world were good, it would often appear with a friendly face
and get stuck in living matter, in poppies, in my blood, in my anger
why leave to someone else what's chasing me
tenderly, long lasting
for touching for calling

step into the together-time of objects, spaces where invisible,
unsolvable problems return with your face.
to say no?
you must take it on. otherwise I'll be unrecognizable.
to say yes?
get ready for the embrace to vanish in delight. pleasure
outshines every rule

the globe made of glass doesn't belong to others, it belongs to me.
the glass-globe is beautiful. joy rules my face. the title of the picture:
the sufferer and his lover. in different roles. in any story, can imagination
be so vivid that it wouldn't remain hidden? you bonded with my heart.
you want to spit a bullet into me

until I center myself in the the world I can't be in the same age
as you, you with your redeemed life,
not until I don't forget beginnings and endings (at least at home),
blind fear smiles back at me: delusion
assumed outside and inside. I'm glamorous and I'm not,
a gorgeous wild horse
—again and again immortals cannot harness me—
then and now do not want me to understand
the difference between being present and the absence of subjectivity
the ornaments of earthly dignities
gee—how many horses do I have to hold back inside me
gee—no turning back
the milky way hangs in my mane

the flue ash in my throat rises to the sky
should I dampen the fire?
hot, a frozen word undresses me,
lets me out and seals the inside

the word thermometer burns my body
knife and rope sing in my mouth
grabbed from the inside to enlist them

hands, how much can I ask you
fire is ~~not~~ fire
mine is ~~not~~ mine

the body grovels on canvas
the reindeer is not tamed
~~what could be~~ taken seriously
this is the plural of time

the previous months want to move here to affect my lines
the once man now child learns to speak, walk and sees
the mother in me (I don't deny it) the sadness of the medial look
repeled and drew me, pampering yet closed off, somehow frayed
us since it is my home and yet not family—shouldn't
separate with words that which could be one

midway between lovemaking and lovemaking
in the cul-de-sac the not-even-beginning ends end
with tiny ends
border fortress warriors, that's how much honor we have received,
hoping for payment, I have to take this story to the market:
the whale of decaying variations, I live too much and the inflation
is high like the sound of the warriors or relatives, like
the bats of happiness: recognize it?
closed snatches of a song for happiness

the knife of yesterday, the knife of my dear snipped my throat
not at all and what one might think of love and death
(rather not hahahahaha) becoming one
what is separable from milk from throat is an illusion –
most-most of it
do not concern me with common names I never was I will be fair
mother tongue of mine: arousals
my blood is red, yesterday concerns you not I love you

your time
I live as an animal
not as a woman
I quickly overlook
the structures there: and I will be badly robed
for what it is
fear/to sit
I need to separate the dress, the age, from the reality of the fabric
The sound of a crying child is overwhelmed by the roar of armed Dactyls.

at the beginning of the story I wrote
that a broken uterus
is a candid heart
though there was no beginning
only a projected ending
where everything is complete and adjoining
when the verbal nouns
splitting and omitting
don't associate with love
and the faded faith foreshadows
the skeleton
well then I will plant flower seeds over here

Gábor G. Gyukics

impossibilism

while running
the whirring of your footsoles
is the silent sound of a cave

the sky is angry
because it can't catch up with you
despite tricks practiced
for hundreds of millennia

only those
who are about to die
can see you

you
down here
with ramrod straight spine
cajole the inexplicable

and when lightning
sleeps
your silence hides
in the thousands of claps
of thunder

nothing indicates
when it
will appear again

visit

broken mirror shards cast shadows
to the boot-sole-dirt covered
ant-covered floor

mosquito and fly reamins stuck
on the wall
faces hidden in the cabinet doors
stare
at the abandoned room

through the window gap
wind fluent in every language
blows secondhand air
at the musty walls

whispers something
to the body-wrinkled bed
waits for no answers
and lashes itself
to the cracks in the door

encyclical

this is the room

its scabrous floor
suggests it's more than just one

sneaking cold
surrounds them

outside

warm replaces the cold
tepid hailstorm swallows the light
washes the air clean

silence dies away
makes our voices
exchange
with routine tasks

tile shards' dust falls from the roof
blinding a staghorn sumac

lost goon stick seen at the Amalfi Coast

the surface of the sea
is warped by the weight of cargo ships
around them the footsteps of Jesus

rain-beaten seagulls follow his path
nibbling on trash and the occasional small fish
confused by the splashing of his feet

gradually
even the largest ship
vanishes into oblivion

your last chance is the fishnet
hanging from the waist of Jesus
forgotten by the children of lost fishermen

a day on earth

the bloody carcass
of the dead dog
that missed the fox
was raided by army of ants

they carried to storage
every morsel
in single file

the poacher
didn't touch the carcass
he trampled on
the anthill

mirage (obsolete)

leaning away from the lectern
she watches
still she can't see
what is before her

her mother buried
the umbilical cord beneath
the only tree in the courtyard
to keep her daughter at bay

the wind takes a break
from her weathered sun-beaten skin
in the empty
mile-wide space

raw air enshrouds
blameless fog-clouds
her skyscraper solitude

his mayfly long life
disperses in the mist
of the cave deep silence

if she could
she'd scatter sand into the eyes
of the thousand-tongued wind

she stays alive
as long as she
laughs
amid the crowd

patch on the foghorn

under the wings of a dead angel
the moon makes love
to the sun
the negative of their bodies
lies on every river bed
mountain range
dirt road
next to your footprint
in every ditch

by the walnut tree
you'll find a piece
of the moon
and neearby
shining beneath
the plum tree
a broken part
of the sun

guardian angels

a pistol is held to your forehead
in a wooded alley of the night

you search for the face behind the hand
as you wait for the click of the trigger
and

instead you see
the hand pull back

you take a deep breath
and when your lungs
are filled with the air of hope
a blow strikes your temple

a stick-up
the thought enters you
together with the pain

two men stand above you
kick your face
your groin
repeatedly
without rushing

one of them leans above you

"you little piece of crap
be happy
you're still
alive"

volumetric analysis

the perfect pronunciation may seem unnatural
as this ostensibly reprimanded formless morning cavalcade
turns into the shapeless day of an awkward evening
lost in the silent doorframe
that leads to a private cloud in a colorful sky
filled with goshawks who call to each other
to point out the plummeting temperature
in the surrounding cities where introverted people
blindsided by authorities ostentatiously lurking around
live off the grid protected by their frozen shells
with no explicable reason that would make them
taintless before the spirits and invented gods
of the inhabitants of this globe

creating your own music

the early troglodytes might have dispised the shindigs of birds
especially the cawing of crows
to beguile the tedium of watching the blunt-edged wedge
as they chopped piece after piece of wood
chasing thousands of mantises and cockroaches from their green caves
they tried to avoid hearing the footfalls of ghosts
by entering someone elses's thoughts
parting the meadow covered with fiddlehead ferns
with the surface of a path shaped by the roots of every tree
they had known which was built long ago across the hills
around a crevasse in the earth
that emitted dense particles of previously inhaled fog
when the thunder slept
they decorated long narrow sticks with tales heard from wildhorses
carved violins out of split wood
glued the pieces together with resin
used the intestines of once-hungry fallen wolves for strings
lifted them to their shoulders
and began to play

Attila Jász

Translated by Gabor G. Gyukics and Thomas Stolmar

Now and Ever

an angel works the camera inside me,
if I knew how to compose music I'd note it down
and give it to Miklós Perényi.
But all I know is to write when silence doesn't work.
Renting a camera is costly on a daily basis,
that's why the angel is using me.
Forcing me to write down what she shows me.
If I don't, she projects the same thing
again, again and again until I give up.

Time-Grey

The real obstacle is the door when the elevator stops on each floor
Will it open or not? Does god want to get in or did he get bored or give up.
The real obstacle is the door at that moment before it opens.

What or who is standing behind it and which floor are we on?
The real obstacle is the door when it closes
Who knows? Are there are more levels?
Or is it simply going back down again as it did before. Countdown...

Opportunity

Anything can be the subject of a poem, my dear M.,
   even the sky above Kapolcs
as it affectedly places itself as a backdrop among the trees above the music
from the stage. Children too, are forgetting everything, dancing to the music
pouring out freely. Only their dogs, despite the excessively
loud music, defy them and lie quietly at their masters' feet,
   feeling they're sheltered there.
Anything can be subject of a poem, my dear M.,
   the calming darkness of trees
on the mountain top, the impossible blue lines of light in the sky,
   unexpected encounters,
or our clumsy motion in the rearview mirror to touch hands
    on the wheel that steers
us home in the dark. At the shoulder of the highway a fawn waits patiently.

Empty

My friends, clean your mirrors this morning
So we might see ourselves in them, shining
The way we should see our true faces every day or
Never more. Tomorrow may be, if we clean this smudged
Empty surface of mirrors. But let's end this year
Today.

The Last Notebook

I always wanted to be a bus driver somewhere in the outskirts
With an empty notebook and a metal lunchbox, sitting on the bench
During break and watching the waterfall. Reading the early poems
Of William Carlos Williams on Sunday mornings. In the evening,

on the pretext of dog walking, I'd slowly drink a pint of beer at the local bar.
Writing a poem, line by line, in my head and if someone asked I'd say,
I'm not a poet; just a bus driver. Now that's real freedom! It exists only
In this notebook or in a film. All other things remain invented stories.

Dream-Mirror

I woke up and an old unfamiliar Indian stared at me from the mirror.
After a while the face became familiar. I recognized my favorite
actor, János Derzsi, I staggered from the bathroom then went back
a few minutes later, hoping the actor had disappeared, but no, in spite
of combing my hair, massaging my face with a towel, opening and closing
      my eyes
he's still there. I go back to bed hoping to wake to something different.
I dream. I'm nobody now.

Abandoned

In my dream I was walking with my love along a beautiful, unfamiliar
        seaside.
Thinking back now it seems it was Italian, the seaside.
Of course, love is eternal, that's why I love the abandoned seaside.

Self-defense

Darkness is an illusion. It's like fear. Evening is
For resting, reading. Lovemaking and/or dreaming.
Man's only enemy is himself. Defend yourself!
And forgive yourself finally. Please.

Relay

Mother, you're sending me signals from the perspective of twenty years
Either I understand or I don't. Naturally it's difficult. You send them
Freely. So we can finally talk calmly. I don't find this weird at all.
Words are no longer necessary. All you have to do is turn
the motion detection lamp on & off at the front door.

The Dream of Being Easy

To be a good poet is not an easy dream. In principle one must
Let things work & flow, not interrupting, asking for the message,
Adding nothing to it. At best, we refine the environment of the text,
Cleaning the picture and with that, oneself as well. Let the inside
Angel say what ever it says or let her go, silent, forcing nothing.
So to be a good poet is not an easy thing, though it is that simple.

Without GPS

(topography)
The frozen crystal constructions in the mall water-pools inside the Bosnian
        pyramid
look exactly like pine trees. According to research, even small amounts of it
can clean & purify polluted water. People have the same hidden pools, called
        hearts
or pomes, but mostly it depends upon topography.

(on the highway at night)
In reality there will be nothing different after death
it will be just as it is in life or in dreams. The same thing will happen
only we'll live in nonlinear time. One can experience
this during a long, monotonous journey. Weariness makes
you let go of your usual space & time barriers, and you're free
just like you will be then.

Dénes Krusovszki

Translated by Gabor G. Gyukics and Duncan Robertson

Austere, Practical

Standing in the crop field, sunk in ankle deep,
I talk, but words aren't reaching you
We walk further, the work progressing
with austere and practical motions.

I send the message in milk,
I translate to rust what I send in leather.
        I'd rather play in the shade like a curious
butcher-boy with a carving knife. I watch you

from over here, forming a deepening impression. I
try hard to imagine when you'll grow cold.
        Of course, it's already begun, it happens,
Everything arrives promptly: chalk, asphalt,

cinder and petroleum jelly. You play with sterile words
while I shout a few cryptic sentences into the jug
        of the afternoon, and fit the lid on carefully.

The Bone Chapel

This wad of damp rag is knotted up on the sagging
clothes line of commemoration, maybe, and bottom-most
sits the unsorted pile of our humiliation.
I'm not apologizing.

I held the camera in my hand
like everyone else. I didn't
tell you to leave after
the tour guide finally stopped talking.

I didn't consider a single one from among
the forty-thousand people whose bones were organized
into rigid ornamentation by František Rint.
By that time, the simple fact of my existance humilated me into dust.

The Source

In the unstoppable melting
you are dragging yourself
along a track of blood
like a deserter from the army,
So, this is the last day of
winter, you mutter, when you
get to the clearing edged
with snowdrops in muddy
patches. The wind still carries
the stench of cadavers.
That would be the past,
clashing branches,
red blotches on white ground.
Then you catch sight of
the deer stepping out
of the bushes and see
the bleeding wound
on its flank when it bends
to quench its thirst
and you lower the gun,
step close, very close.
So, this is source of my future.
It looks at you then
and says: *Yes.*

Elegy Sound

Without detour, like a rocket,
We proceeded towards lucency,
We didn't hold each other any differently
Than people who grab the rough handles
Of shopping baskets.

I wanted to tell you this before,
When the song of the granary
Was overwhelming every other sound.
Now, before harvest, we're in the position
Of not having sown anything.

I still remember that the water tasted
Strange from the spout of the tin kettle,
Everyone who went to the well offered it
To one another, testing whose was best,
And frankly, that was enough for us.

Yesterday

A beekeeper might look
inside an empty hive
once he understands
that its family
will never return.

The Second

The cock with the slit throat
stood suddenly up, left the enamel saucepan
full of his blood, the knife dropped
into the grass and the basin filled with hot water
and started running backwards in the yard.
You could see his lopped-off head
slapping against his side with every step
and you wondered whether he
saw anything while he ran.
Then you remembered Lazarus from
Bible class where all they talked
about was resurrection.
Yet he has to die again
and the second time is for keeps.

Back

Before we begin eating dinner
he takes the knives and forks from us,
stacks the porcelain plates
and shuts it all back in the cupboard.
He nips morsels from our supper,
separates the flour and the eggs,
the breadcrumbs and the meat,
lets the juice back into muscle fibers,
places meat back on the bones,
stretches sinew from joint to joint,
assembles the body parts,
pours blood back into veins,
heaps guts back into the abdomen,
knits nerve fibers together,
puts the tongue in the mouth, the eyes in the skull,
heart behind the ribs,
sets skin back over the chest,
takes the carving knives from our hands,
wipes them assiduously cleans of blood.
Then he retires to the background
and watches as we begin to eat.

1990

The light air, of course,
but the overripe sigh riven
from the vinyl floor covering
in the decontaminated rooms
of the mountain sanitarium
is more memorable.

Waiting for something
to move on the balcony,
looking at the woods.
Cold light from a lamp among
motionless branches of dead evergreens.

Later, an evening game around the chairs
placed in the middle of the restaurant,
and the salt of an unexpected defeat,
like a statement misinterpreted, where
whoever stands up
can't sit back down, and those
who remain seated remain alone.

Letter

Thanks, you later wrote,
not waiting for me, like someone
who has reached a break in the air
between two fog banks and
understands what she's looking at
before she actually sees it.
You went on to say
we'd end up in a rear-view mirror,
our existence compressed
into nervous waving
and the jerking of the steering wheel,
because it's all in vain,
hurrying and begging.
Those who lie on the asphalt
won't ever get up,
those who turn their heads
and who, when given a rattle,
will shake it until they faint.

The Visit

You can't trust birds.
You repeated that phrase
when I visited you.
Otherwise you silently watched the park
lined with trees steadily
flinging off their rusty-yellow leaves.
I thought you were going to say
something about the weather
when you turned back around,
but instead you softly repeated,
You can't trust birds.
I wish I knew what you
wanted with that half-finished sentence.
You could have, at least,
explained it to me then.
I might have stayed longer,
but it made me leave
because I missed you most
when we were together.

Gábor Lanczkor

Translated by Gabor G. Gyukics and Duncan Robertson

Caravaggio

Paint it again. Those hypocrites wanted me
To paint another to replace the first
Because it was obscene. What's obscene about it
Is how the grace of the Holy Spirit moves inside us.
And yet we are dumbstruck,
Paralyzed hicks, an angel floating overhead.

Straining, the word of God in our throats the way the rapids' stones
Tear rushing mountain streams into branches,
The ship's bow cuts deftly through the waves. We didn't dock
In Gaeta. Creaseless, the canvas sail dazzled us, as if pulled tight
                over a stretcher.
Blood red compass needle stabbing a wound in my back,
Our ship aimed duplicitously north before a southwester,
A wild notion seized me: I would picture this blaze
As a realm conquered by my prophecy, these two worlds overlaid.,
How might I ever dispossess myself of such an idea?
I slept armed to the teeth, if one can call that brief nightly torment sleeping,
Leaning against rank tow-sacks with vermin searching restlessly behind them.
Early morning, I went up on deck to get some fresh air.
Fizzling stars in the salty mist, a rumble in the east, followed
            by a fast sunrise, virulent
Translucent stirrings beneath the cover of the rippling waves—
After we landed in Porto Ercole
Around noon
I was helped to the pier
And went in search of a tavern
Or somewhere I could hide from the heat.
When I returned to the port to get my things,
I could not see my ship anywhere.
That badly-paved town was a paper-thin hull
Over an airless swamp. Only two palm-sized spots
On its surface among cleft basalt stones were pure ground,
where shapeless dragon lizards snatched at me with

steaming claws, then dissolved into the damp heat.
Merisi turned blond immediately, a genius from the north,
Your self-portraits all belong to doubt.
By the time I reached Rome
The walled city was unrecognizably changed.
I saw huge building sites in place of narrow streets, palaces,
squares and churches. Fenced with wire, immense frames
of high rises stood illuminated by spotlights in the night.
The empty river bank was overgrown with weeds.
It was as if a hurricane
had pulled the proletarian neighborhood
on the other side to pieces. As if it were reassembled again
by the ongoing storm, and the push and pull of God and men
and animals had created new mechanisms from its buildings and streets
and squares for my delirium to ruin and pug. Beyond everything
in this panicky self-assessment of human life
I now die.

Byron Burns Shelley's Body on the Seashore

I.

I was about to eat supper
when I was called for: they had found him.
I wasn't expecting a pretty corpse.

I tried to keep up with the rushing
messenger despite my lame foot.
It was Satan fresh from heaven

drowned in the ocean, not some junior god
with wounded knees—that's what I read
on the darkening faces around

the waterlogged body through the smoke of torches.
The scream on his distorted greenish-blue face
reminded me of an icon hacked with Turkish swords

I had seen once in an Orthodox monastery. His
eyelids and lips open only a crack—
cruel waves, screeching metal, engine noise.

I saw the protracted crash in the tumult of the ocean,
Gods hiding in
frictional rumbling noise

and in those shaped according to their own image
from which our facsimile monsters were born
among inert lumps of time.

Dark
the sea foamed behind me,
the torches fluttered and sizzled.

2.

I made a fire from dry pine branches.

Three representatives from the city wouldn't allow
the gruesome corpse
to enter the town of Spezia
due to the danger of contamination.

Like Solomon
leaning over to the soft breasts of Sheba,
I undressed him and was surprised by his cleanness.

His seaborne aura
confidentially revealed itself,
decay radiating from beneath his clothes.

And, while the nest-shaped, resin-scented pile
caught, crackling, the scorched feathers
of that blond phoenix began to stink
insufferably, exclaiming
the futility of our lives—
Abstractions. You open a friend's chest to get to his heart.

The enigmatic design of his lung lobes
catches your eye through the manifold river
of musculature around his heart

You'd swim into your common future, a seer—
from where in vain you'd both look back on the tide-licked sand
and again, see no one there.

The sea, the rising sun, holds this unpunctuated infinity together
the way glue holds the spine of a book.

3.

In each pocket of his raglan, left and right

Lay a drenched book.
I kept them both
until recently, here in Greece I somehow lost them.

Hand

The art piece titled
Double Negative
is located in Moapa Valley
Nevada.
They dug
two nine-meter-wide, fifteen meter deep,
        four hundred fifty-seven meter long trenches
opposite each other
on both sides
of a natural canyon.
Most of the two hundred forty-four thousand tons
        of sandstone and rhyolite had to be hauled out.

Strips were cut
        from smooth layers of papyrus reed stem
Then, after soaking them in water
        they were placed on top of each other
creating lattice
which was struck with a wooden hammer until it stuck fast.
When it dried,
it was burnished,
        and as a hawk flies over a zoo
        that's how the scribe's hand glides above it

Triple Negative

Fires burning down at the lake
are visible from here, but not the men
who burn the reeds.

Along the stripped sides of Hegyestu
deep in its basalt heart
the wind-packed snow
is glossy white.

Three extinct volcanos.
there volcano tops removed:
Hegyestu, Ság, Badacsony—
like the Chain Bridge or the Parlament Building.

                          Edifying.

The indentations on them are elementary—
like a pair of disassembled scissors

                          their silhouettes.

Along the stripped sides of Hegyestu
deep in its basalt crevice
the wind-packed snow
is glossy white.

Fires burning down at the lake
are visible from here, but not the men
who burn the reeds.

Rembrandt van Rijn: Self-portrait at the Age of Sixty-three

My face's future is without hands.
I fold them. Hide them in my gloves.
My face's future. It's hard to grasp.
This is the only real mission

for all my tiniest cells. Let them speak
to the dead circuits of my twenty
or twenty-six-year-old body. To the fact
that you wake with me early in the morning.

Or for another moment now.
If at all. If no one else. If the debt
is nobody else's. Then to whom is it owed, and how much.

And now he's died. Hurry up. Be quick. Dress up.
He isn't here; that or it's the dawn of a golden age,
No grief.

The Second Coming

Like from the babe's stomach
that sour smell
of coughed-up mother's milk
this how the
                    newborn
yells with gums.
Not bitter,
hungry,
                    for the lion is born with teeth,
and the gums of the oracle are bare as those of hundred-year-old men.
Its body is in the maternal body, and already its head freely
                                        predicts.

The Violin

To István Fried

Remembering not forgetting:
Forgetting not remembering.
The way the Irish learn Irish again,
the way I forget my German —
the kind of insincerity with which a nearly prodigious child
                    plays the violin at the end of his first school year:

Remembering, not forgetting:

The way the Irish will never learn Irish again —
insincerity:

If there is a synagogue, do not speak Hebrew.
Do not listen to Hebrew
outside of a synagogue.
Forgetting, not remembering.

Julia Lázár

Translated by Gabor G. Gyukics and Belinda Subraman

For a Birthday

The invisible bridge between us
Tends to be there even when the wind blows
When another foot stamps on it, when the
Weight of steps sways it to and fro

I can't imagine a time, a space
That would hold me without you
Now it matters not who did what for
And against it, quarter of a century.

The bridge squeaks between us.
The weight of our ages won't tear it down
For we won't be at either end of it when
It spins weightlessly in space.

Colors

You know, they count as tiny things,
the way you kiss my shoulders.
The light touch becomes heavy,
holds me back when I'd push you away
to keep you for eternity.
Strawberries smile at me from a bowl.
I think of you with a blue coffee cup.
Is that proper on an average day
while red blood flows in the world
and yellow roses bloom in the garden?

Ophelia

A scent pervaded her,
the scent of a flower.
She dove into waves,
was neither alive nor dead.
Many were happy for life
but not for her.
Water flowers fondled her,
never-embracing arms.
History is a nightmare
from which I'm trying to wake.
Through passing time
the soul is a jackal
and elders with big heads
ask you: Why?

Poem Without Title

History is a nightmare
from which I am trying to awake,
—James Joyce

Through your passing time
'the soul is a jackel
and large-headed eldders
ask you: Why?

That is the Prettiest

I didn't go to cure others in Africa
I didn't learn to play the piano
I didn't become the sweetheart of
any earl, a count, or a diplomat

I placed the applecore on the furniture.
The list of my other sins is infinite
because I hated it if they stipulated
how I could, in an instant, ruin my life.

What is prettiest is boundless pleasure.
It's there on the faces of children
but harshness ends exactly
where pleasure and death are kin.

Lullaby (Ditty)

Between blue and dark velvet sky
the sun and the moon exchange dresses.
I have a place up there at their party
but I travel through and to the ground.
To put my heart and words in order,
to stop fear from going any further,
make the velvety sky a bit softer.
Instead of me, a star greets you
and covers you with a cupola of light.

Triangle

The foliage flashes for a second
through a triangle-shaped rift. That's life:
The way the eyes reflect the light,
feels joy sensing its green nuances.
Then the sun shifts and the shadow with it.
What the spectator thought was infinite
turns dark. Only craving remains
and the auster scent of dust.

Living Monument

The columns are already standing. The square is ugly.
They're building a monument to the ineptitude,
the shame, proving there isn't remembrance,
only greed for power, struggle, and hate.

Torches at the feet of cordons,
photographs, books, a torn Bible,
faces, stories. This is what remains
because we're human and alive.

The wind blows, rain washes words away.
At the rear, wide-eyed uniformed men startle
if someone looks them in the eye

and sings. We'll remember for him,
for them. Stones crumble away.
Moss grows on the fallen angel.

Red Oak

Like a red oak, only a small part of it
visible in the tight cropping of the picture,
in the unrealistically-red flux,
the past swirls in a maelstrom of sunburnt leaves.
A role comes out of the role reversal.
A leaf falls from the treetop
that very second in time.

Color matters, the strength of whirling,
particles are needed, the origin
miniscule in the unmeasurable,
the human value in the divine

Footnote

The wand is broken, Prospero is dead.
He died because he didn't stay on the island.
Perhaps he didn't know that power is not enough
for those who made magic only once.
Ariel is alive because she is a free spirit,
and the hero of our age is Caliban again.
A disgusting, fallen ruler
or a miserable and loathed fool,
dangerous because he wants power,
the girl, the sound of the island
only for himself, because he feels
contempt for others, because he thinks
he is the heir and can do anything
on the island. In the mirror of fear
he is pretty.

Mónika Mesterházi

Translated by Gabor G. Gyukics and Belinda Subraman

When I Thought

If love were like flu virus and I could give
some of it to every poverty-stricken man,
despite whatever amount remained with me
there would still be too much indifference
in the world to make it work.
It's a little bit like that,
but flu is much more altruistic. Not waiting for
compensation, it doesn't take advantage of anything
(what's not enough for some is plenty for others).
True that it passes most of the time and suffering
is more during than after. The flu is similar,
after all, to love in only one unfortunate thing:
I pass it on to those I love.

Exactly the Opposite

Exactly the opposite of the blind,
I depend on my sight and don't
stumble all the time.
There are additional advantages.
For example, I'll find money on the ground
and I won't let anyone to push me around.

But if hubris comes and I look at the sky,
or a faulty presumption blinds me,
or the so-called eyes of the mind
look at something for themselves—
the fate of friends, my situation,
people who scramble,
or how over time
men became such morons—

then the tiniest glance at the ground is enough.
I pay for my hubris on the cobblestones,
torn stockings and shredded pant knees
help me understand the fate of my ancestors.
I'll patch the pants or throw them away,
I'll fix self-pity as well.
And for a while I'll be watchful
then start all over again.

Denial

touched
a certain degree of freedom
caught
some faith
redeemed
some pleasure

cursed the local machos
the gynecologists
and caused pain
on every occasion
once in half a year

went down to change money
wait for him he said
pushed me into the room
with his moneyed hands
tried to start me
like I was
a winter car

I'd believed
he was so smart
spoke his mother tongue
better than I

yet it wasn't enough
he obviously had no idea
about my things
when he intervened
he talked about
how one should live better
then it dawned on me
that he too was in denial

and that ended it with him
no need for disproval

Cold

The windstorm tore an opening to the unheated room
and left it open. Cold air blew in through the crevice
for days. What was that whitethroat doing there?
A migratory bird in winter, it lay in front of the balcony
door with dull eyes. Its body was cold
as its tilted head rested in my palm.
How much unthinkable evil suddenly filled
the heated rooms? The rigid impotence of shoulders and neck
reveal irritation and anger in every motion, in this pretty
songbird that could hide under a single green leaf
in summer. That this black-capped, fluffy-feathered guest
appeared is a tiny unexpected source of joy, but we saw it late.
It lies silently on the cold threshold.

Cold Front

I aged several years
the night
I awakened,
rain falling,
as homeless.
I'd planned to perform
a monologue
in a play,
but I didn't have the script,
I'd left it home.
I couldn't read,
I went to the park.
There was no way
to call anyone.
The telephone
was out of order.
There was nothing left
 to do but wake up
and remember
previously considered
options for my future
and try to figure out why
I had found myself
in that sweet-sounding
word: *homeless.*

Stromovka

A tiny-palmed maple leaf
Paddles sideways through the air
Slides forward, paddles fast
with its stem, slides and descends

Havlíček Gardens

The sun opens on
a garden of valleys,
there is a separate night
under the yew trees.

In a Bank in Budapest

You would have loved that scene
in the bank when the bankteller said,
There are exactly ten years between us.
I suddenly didn't know what to answer,
I hope it was a good ten years,
I said finally. In the meantime,
while working on the withdrawal,
How about you, she asked.
Did your ten years go well?
Yes, I think so. Later, when I saw
my face reflected in a window display,
it occurred to me what else
I could have said: *I could*
look much better than I do.
But it was something for her
to speak with me. You would have liked
that scene if it had happened in time.
A few weeks before, I could have told you.

Year 2016

I was in the middle of two tasks but I sat down
in the company of trees and birds on the balcony
for a bit and I'd melted into the landscape
when a car, engine roaring, stopped.
The driver carried tools in and out for a long time.
Eventually he sat back with a small propane bottle
and tried his lighter to see if it was working.
While he unloaded the toolboxes I'd already felt
my back and the wrinkles on my face stiffening,
as if my grandmother were sitting there.
I didn't want to see what I was watching
I didn't want to know what I knew. I hoped
we wouldn't blow up just yet. I drank my coffee
and set back to work at my table.

Here I Sit

Here I sit with earplugs and drink
my morning coffee amid noise
and ropes hanging in front of the window.

Workers insulating the house
stand on a long boardwalk
or on a suspended board.
A railing is under the line of their groins.

They lean out and the resistance of the drill
sometimes shifts them
away from the concrete wall.

Because the ropes swing,
they get closer then further away,
drilling up to the tenth floor, even in the dark.

At least my ears are plugged.
They should wear hard hats.
I draw the curtains so I don't see them.

Zita Murányi

Translated by Gabor G. Gyukics and Michael Castro

Csepel Island

small snow-white boats
row along the stars in the night
tense lines of dark walls shine
csepel shines

like a spine in the center of the river
the water waves around you, knows not
how to handle your body as it oozes into dreams
the embankment of Buda and the moon

are carried away by the dark sheet of water
which finds itself face to face
with the depth written on the sky
you cover your back with the night
not knowing the reason you sweat

Bosnyák Square

the steeple of the bosnyák square church
remains the only landmark in this gray
roundabout the sky is a mysterious toy
of fog, the rain dismantled by chain
reactions of clouds only the white
stripe of the crosswalk looks slushy,
as if we still walk knee-deep,
in the month of February

spring boulevards are blooming
the silvery forehead of metal
sparkles on the cross indicating
that this will be the night
when pain is nailed to the moon
a few rays decompose on the sidewalk
and just as on your arm a red blotch shows
the cupping of the day
its arm is damp as well

Sidewalk

I still don't know which way I'll be walking
the town looks familiar, the walls look familiar
those two perfect strangers in the middle of the street
are the motion with which fresh cement
is mixed with gravel

and the sky above them with its separated concavity
as if it would split into clouds
at times like this fresh concrete is still pitch black
the sidewalk becomes gray gradually

the two men are stiff as ramrods
only their spines might lean to the right
in this March wind. Standing next to each other
they waver at the same time
like the concrete in their shovels.

Terebesi Square

perhaps what bothers me and that black jaybird
at terebesi square is that the broken windows
in the number three tram are like fast wings
and as they're flapping past I feel the jeans
become much colder against my knees

the trees stand ramrod straight
and this wrinkled morning is
like a silver colored bracelet
you can almost hear it rattling
as the gray husk slips down
a couple inches on the trunk

the brown bark becomes visible again
and stockinged knees slowly
pull through the hole on your jeans
the color is black as soot, as the
twitter stuck in the beak of a bird
when the light is swallowed

Four Meters

slowly the walls will get an orange tint
and light will sparkle inside
the lampshades in Pest
Buda is still in darkness
the Danube is such a blue

above the two halves of the city
the sun scatters its yellow rays
making him patriarch of the sky
the clouds are separating

below the February sky the way gray
waves lean on each other as white haired elders do
you lean on the rail backing the water and wonder
how everything belonging to this endless night
reflected in the four-meter window of a tram
will gradually disappear.

It Didn't Come Up Yet

I've visited copenhagen, new york
a seal-skinned man begged on the platform
they said there weren't any poor people there
a light brown man from Florida left fingerprints on my shoulder
we watched the gray concrete in front of the store
where flagstone hung onto flagstone

the plastic code on the label of the coke bottle
was pressed by four palms
to turn it to chump change
how many times does the sun
set over the transatlantic
in europe it hasn't risen at all
still the light's dropped to its knees billions of times on its rays

Flood

when I carry you under my heart way too long
        you get ragged like a worn t-shirt
you're even missing from my nightmares
        the trees turn their trunks away I don't know
if god is madder at me or you if I cover my head with a plastic bag
        like the old ones do will I at least understand
why you don't love me I rustle with every step
        like autumn when it wrinkles the fallen leaves
beneath our feet the leaves don't crunch
when clouds pour rain down on my skin
        does the passing thunderstorm soothe your warm skin
when you become a rainbow will you color me
        with every dried up drop
since you don't believe in the flood anyway

That Boy

If I could only forget that
boy at the South Railway Station
his ragged clothes had a permanent stench
he tells me to buy him an ice cold Coke
it would be good at any vendor across the way
he carries hidden countries on his back
how many underpasses reeking with urine are carried in that backpack
should I look into his eyes or with blossoms in my mouth
whisper that I have a striped straw with me

as he drank he digested every word I said
I could have turned aside whispered to his dark brown
mouth that I had no change at all
I don't really know what I said to his empty palm
how much clatter stalled in bottles
he sipped it fast with disgust and delight
a sickening taste on his tongue as in the depth
of the sips bubbles banded together

If only... those hands and broken shoes
coal-colored clothes wrapped around the body
the sizzling concrete, those tracks orthogonal curves
I exist for nothing if he can't ask anything from me
and suddenly I feel the undying thirst
that boy feels in the roof of my mouth
where that unquenchable pain lays shingles
to make me call out to passers-by

I was told three hours for the anesthesia to wear off

Glory

angelic laughter was heard from the endless flow
of silence though it was only the wind that swept
through the decade-old trees and branches
lost some leaves from their spring stock there were
a few mouth-shaped leaves resembling smiles among
those the wind knocked down yet the street wasn't
awakened by these rather introverted smiles
the moon's face overlapped the first few rays of sun
I thought they were standing right behind me closing
the wings none knew they had for they were invisible
behind their bodies as they stood in the wind yet it seemed
like levitation as I heard as the inner glory of the trees
knocked down then raised in every age-ring above their heads

Sea

what lures the drunken boat of the pupil
to the sea of another eye if the surging
and drifting circles of the sea
did not sound an alarm for her
to shipwreck her again

if I see black flag on a house
I imagine that same black canvas
stretched across the heart filtering
staggering heartbeats through the ventricles
not one but two nights' pain
beneath my fingertips
from the flotsam and jetsam of the soul
a piece of god to someone

Autumn

with the darkness before creation
during infinite but starlit evenings
the universe kneels on the floor
in autumn's fallen leaves.

Shard

order broke inside me I dance
on shards but I'm a heavy curse
like the world I lose a billion years
from my volume per minute

Zsuka Nagy

Translated by Gabor G. Gyukics and Terri Carrion

two in the street

as a finale he threw a chair to the middle of the rundown bar,
he wanted to throw two, but they held him down.

it was a cheesy, faceless place, a Pepsi-ad-color eclectic poverty.
dawn and blue and shit-colored flowers bloomed at the edge of the city.
they were standing on their own two feet pushing each other the way they
played with their dump trucks, ragdolls and pillowcases
            in childhood, and later with the thrown-out clothes of their lovers.

but now, Villonesque in their loathsomeness, ready to steal and destroy.
they eat the moon at night, fried eggs they say. it's enough for them.
fuck reality and mix the moon with hard liquor,
street-smell incense, mint cigarettes that they bite, rip and tear.
they cannot compare the stars, become uneasy, start scratching
the pimples on their bodies, stars they say, and calm down.

sitting in a booth at Gajdos' Bar, they feel cold, moon already gobbled up, need
                        something solid.
they stand, sway like trees in the wind. bony, their skin hangs like stretched
t-shirts, but it's starry they say, then drop as their skin turns to urine and
vomit-like goo.

in their dreams, they have their own table and freely take.
their blouses and shirts are ironed, their jeans are clean, their shoes shine
there's a roof above their heads, simple small rooms and everyone minds
their own business, things only they know, ain't drunk they say, clinking their
            tall glasses like it's some holiday or other happy event or just because.

two people in the street, easily transplantable, lie on a kind of asphalt rug
go wild like grown children, know they are only similes and metaphors.
they rise, cut the throat of reality, put on their disguises,
walk in blue and shit-colored eclectic poverty in the gypsy alley
then put all of it in writing.

bandage week

home is what you can never go back to
home is where you fell yesterday
where you didn't answer the phone
home is where you were raving
where you were taken to the hospital from
home is where you grew old
where you knew where everything was
if the nurse asks if you've had anything to eat
you answer that you have food at home
or if you're told you must eat
you say you'll eat at home
home is mortar-ground infusion medicine
home is where you're not drugged
where you were able to stand up
where you were able to speak
home is where you can never go again

bike path two

the countryside's sitting in flip-flops on worn sofas at the back of the house
preserving plums, peaches, tomatoes in the summer kitchen,
discarded furniture, wine casks, gourds, Csepel camping bicycle,
      and porcelain knick-knacks in the shed

onion smell blown by the wind, cat urine and pigsty stink rule the yard
the grandkids bathe in washbowls, eat thick slices of bread with pork
      drippings made by their grandma's black hands

old women wait at an abandoned railway station, kitchen garden herbs in
      their sacks
looking frightened by the world, asking for help in adjusting the sacks on
      their backs

the countryside lives by habitual motion, people help and kill with the same
      gesture
sometimes they don't ask for sausage or challah but murder

the old ones rake the earth, pull weeds even as they die
the countryside sits in flip-flops at the back of the house
on plastic chairs thrown out from small cafés
where plaster flaked away, the lights have burned out, the pork drippings are
      ready on the stove
nothing hurts, *grab a hoe*, dawn cries a few drops of rain, and the homeland
is hung on the line to dry.

country man, report poem

I'd smoke all the world's tobacco, then stuff fog in my cigarettes, he adds.
he has hardly any, his son will bring more tomorrow. the great plain is bluish-
       green in his eyes,
the whites of the Puli's eyes peek through dreadlocks, it barks as he leans
on his sheep-hook and watches the flock,
how the face and hand of civilization ruin the land, terra incognita,
man isn't the faithful companion of man but of the animals, the dog, the
flock. this vastitude. he points at the infinite boundary that he walks every
day. *nye kupity,* I read while he croaks and coughs, hitting his legs as he sits in
the wagon near a stove with just an ice cold chunk of white bread on top.
how can anyone be so poor and so happy? he looks at me—it's my flock and
my bible—puts his jacket on, the fog from his cigarette becoming more and
more dense.

since I've loved you I've brushed my teeth twice
a day, made the bed in the morning, leisurely
pulled on clean socks, no sweat.
since I've loved you, I've hardly been late anymore.
I've told my bike *slow down.*
Rosalie, since I've loved you I've been willing to leave
Europe with you, pull my rooted feet out
if you can, since I've loved you the stars fell on
Earth, they are jewels on your sweet shortcake
coaster body since I've loved you I don't remember
anything, I've never loved anyone in shameful poppy
fields but since I've loved you I know it's possible to step
from One to Two and then Two becomes One

m6

since I've loved you happiness doesn't tire me anymore
lonesomeness won't remove my covers at night
we are one room one pier one poem
since I've love you I've known
every love has tragedies
sometimes nothing is better than something
it's easier to destroy good than fix bad
since I love you I haven't minded getting out of line
I don't mind that I'm an albatross
since I've loved you I haven't been a daydreamer
my heart is a red comic book because
I'm not worried about how long this poem
can be written in happy lines

mio

since I've loved you its stopped raining, ambulances
run shrieking through the city, their throbbing
palm-size lights pumping blood up against black sky,
since I've loved you, you've often asked me if I believed
what is happening now with you would have happened
with someone else, you've confronted me with the past, how many
times should I deny my past for you, I've confessed in a poem
an infinite desire to deny it before my mother, ashamed
before my father, heart effusion—heart vomit—heart ejection,
the whale spewing Jonah out, the past spewing the old
one out, since I've loved you I haven't told you how I've ended everything,
how I've screwed everything up when things were great, took care not
only of me but of you too because I've made myself
forget you, be every timeline for me in this giant selfishness,
in my selfish oasis, want me if I do too, love me if I do too,
be yet a woman a man the way I am, who he or she was you are, who
was your she or he, one in the past who leaves like a cloud,
trading places and the world grows up to us.

trek 1: heart camera

you are the carbon fiber in my bicycle
you put grease on my chain repair my gears
you keep me inside Mondays
the way the spokes keep up the wheels
your prism eyes show me the way
in my flat tires you are the glue
clean water in the basin making the puncture visible
the smudge the blotch the spoke-bone fracture
the bruise under my eye is all you

immortality

dad is a shell
mom is a fuzzy tap root
when rain comes we're drenched together
when the sun shines we're together
in the light

sometimes I bury them in the woods
to save them from trouble
I call them to hold hands,
whisper in each other's ears

dad and mom are whispering,
earth is guarding them,
we practice resurrection,
they come out of the ground,
wash their bodies,
dress and go to work

they call me on Sunday saying
lunch will be ready on Wednesday,
they ask if I have anything to eat,
then I invite them to the woods again.
they say it's awkward for them
but they'll do it if I want to

Márió Z. Nemes

Translated by Gabor G. Gyukics and Duncan Robertson

The Breasts of Pushkin

1. They are touching each other. They smack on suction cups. I'm not saying I'm sensual, just a man. Here they peel off their genitals the way my mother exfoliates her aching breasts. Does anyone come here for regular chemical peels? Pushkin is being welded in this factory. The three brothers are knocking him together pretty well. Pushkin wants to be a woman, but his chest is too firm.

2. Dance is a greasy machine. Hanging by a ligament or some other gymnastic apparatus. Everybody is lubed up with happiness. This is the last enema before love. I don't want to end up watching old men but that's what happens every night by eight.

3. I brought a glowworm that loves grease. I'll slip it into the ear of a girl who still speaks Russian. Then I might hear better, although that wasn't me in Onegin. I respect body culture because I too occasionally lie down in wrapping paper and say I'm a gift.

4. The three brothers don't have good breasts but there are other mutations. Don't poke the protuberances of my love. If they start flowing and you're stuck, bobbing up and down in vain, there will be no one left who remembers. There are stones and women's things in the riverbed. We push each other through the muck.

5. They are pestering my worm. I might have replaced it already. With a triangle maybe, though, they can see everything. But not out from between thighs. No apologies, they want milk from Pushkin.

6. My mother's breasts were made in this factory too. She was still a drummer-girl when they were made. I think she had a good job, could do it even while dancing. She didn't date Russians but wrote letter after letter to my father. Why do they speak formally? That's not normal at all.

7. One of the three brothers is always wailing. While they do it, he howls. He wants to be made a gift for the other two, but they're only interested in men. I go back to the body, into the milk. There are no worms in it because it's milk from the east. I want to be like Onegin after he's been scraped by a curette.

Evening Milk

People threw money in his hat and the man let them
touch his hump.
Then he squeezed milk from it, but it was too cold,
and the kids didn't want any,
yet it would have been no more
than stuffing peppers
with darkness and meat.
Before sleep
the stuff of life conceals itself, and in the end
one hand washes the other: what's not in man
no man can produce.

Red Water

In the village of the dwarves, everyone is three inches tall. Those taller than three inches are shot, for which they have a special pistol. It's called Mother's Wrath, but sometimes they also find time to work with a saw. Diligent folks for sure. They have a queen, but no other women. The queen's name is Suzy. She lives in a cottage the color of bile in the center of the village (the dwarves lick her door handle every evening). Once, it just so happened that a wandering student, who was more than three inches tall, found his way to the village. The dwarves gathered around him and stared hungrily at his hands. The boy had nice hands and could imitate animals with them, which especially irritated the dwarves, because all they did was collect bones. The nimbleness of his fingers charmed Suzy, who sighed deeply in her bile cottage. Let's unleash Mother's Wrath on him, the dwarves begged the queen, but she refused since it would have meant being transported into the body of the wandering boy, forever. The dwarves went skulking through the pet cemetery, hanging their heads, not knowing on what to take out their pain, so picked flowers from the graves instead, but Suzy was already the boy's. Well, let this day be a day of anger. If Mother is dead, let Father give birth to sons. They surprised the wandering student in his sleep and carved the flesh from his bones. The dethroned queen wept in her bile cottage and, instead of tears, red water poured out all night.

Artaud's Leather Jowls

You can't sleep inside Artaud's mummy.
There's almost no room or air. For lack of anything better
we gobble up teenage garbage to survive.
But this is self-defeating, since Artaud
was so thin by the time of his death,
that we can chew through
the dry husk that remains. Naturally, this may also cause problems,
like if we prematurely vomit up the undigested mass,
further reducing the space available to us.
In such a moment we can only laugh, like at grape-harvest
when processed juice is separated from its carcass and turned into
bittersweet nectar. In such a moment,
Artaud weeps, and visitors say,
an angel watches over him!
We are many, a real rat kingdom.
We are not in the least bit respectful, we scratch out our eyes
if someone winks instead of nods.
Nowadays it happens in the best families,
especially those without the guts for
slave porno. Still, we're not disappointed. We're fidgeting
in parallel and in tandem, sometimes like
a piledriver
other times rowdy. Artaud is dancing!
We're trying to move these old boots.
Polka and jitterbug, this is how the plague razzle-dazzles in the east!
Not that there's enough skin left on our faces, but that too
follows from the problem previously discussed, according to which
our possibilities are limited by the physical condition
of his prepared corpse. But
everything is more fun in Artaud's skin!
Let the good doctors go mad and run headless
through the corridors of the Anatomy Museum when the
intestinal-music plays, that means we have chewed a hole in his libido.
We don't want to be intelligent, which would be no easy task

since no more than a few of us can fit in the cranial cavity, moreover
it's always colder in there, but in our opinion,
it's the hypnosis act of the century.

The Archbishop Starts to Weep

They baked the Sultan's head in the imperial furnace,
until it was crunchy and European. But they couldn't
braise out all its Eastern character.
By the time he was ready and muscular hands had removed him from the
        oven, tongues had begun to wag, and everyone wanted to reach
inside the coal black harem of his skull. Manly power radiated from the
        stump of his neck and all
the boys hurried round, mesmerized as the procession set off toward
the inners rooms of the palace where the archbishop sat in agitation.
The Hungarian is hungry! – shouted the privy counselor,
to obliterate the ruler he was to obliterate.
The tables were laid with silver utensils, harp music danced through the air
        from a screened-off chamber, and there was a swan, too,
led by two pageboys in love, but who, in two days' time,
would garotte each other on the feather-strewn floor of the birdhouse.
The archbishop looked at the head and his internal organs turned to jelly.
The aristocratic head smelled like a little bird roasted with its mother stuffed
        inside.
Francis thought of his own mother and of cannons. He began to sweat with
        anticipation:
he hadn't imagined that he might, here and now, find a best friend.
He would have liked to immediately penetrate and begin sucking clean the
        cranial cavity, that man-pit which offers itself through the thick fog
of Constantinople. Francis had never been, but had always felt that the Sultan
        was his brother and now he came to him in such crunchy regalia
because Hungarian men are so alone.

Bauxite

There haven't been clean girls in the village since sediment from the bauxite mines was washed into the western valleys by rain. Every morning the men from the swamp go to their artesian wells where they are unable to clean their horns. There is nothing to wash the girls with either. They wander over the soccer field with bile-colored lips and an old woman throws dried clay at them if they try to leave the fenced-in pitch. This is the age of hydras, whispers the forester. The town steward pokes an animal's ass with a stick, but instead of stiff flesh he finds a mucus filled sack. My dad won't come out of the garage anymore. There's just enough room to slide bowls of soup under the door, which he spits out through the window. I keep his broken teeth in a garden basin. Occasionally, I build a hospital from them or I place one under my tongue and say, *Happy birthday*. At the end of May, the young men gather behind the pig dispenser in white shirts, their faces smeared with pure mud. It's a production drill, they reassure their relatives from the city. The decorated animals are driven before tractors, bells and rocks, while a cantor flaggelates the men with stinging nettles. This festive parade reaches the sand mine, where the chosen one cuts off the women's hair and stacks it in a pile. The cantor sets the stack on fire. Some of the townies try to take pictures and are chased away by swamp kids with rugged limbs. The smell of burning hair inundates the entire region, and my dad begins to retch. He spits his loose teeth into a basin, but smiles, as if they were pulled out by the hand of an intelligent being. This is death by bauxite, nothing more.

Communicating Vessels

The girl picked at random
is quiet, can't let me go.
Her favorite word is: *ear-conch*.
She lives in a sublet and leaves
the light on when she goes
running in the evenings when
they pour asphalt.
Sometimes she has a mouth
around her tit, that's
only a hunch. She is writing
a homework assignment on
communicating vessels.
The grease that drips
between its sequence of diagrams
hurts her eyes and makes her dizzy.
She goes down to alpha, but
someone is already there.
In the room behind the ear
a laid table is out, waiting for
hungry friends. The girl
clutches her name inside herself, then
as she is tapped on the back,
must say good-bye to everything
in a hurry. Sitting in front of the TV,
I feel her hair growing inside my head.
Stroking me from the inside,
but occasionally I throw it up.
That's when I see the strange mouth
pouring out asphalt in dark cones.

Steering Wheel

I'd like a hand all my own, so I could point out things with it. But I'm not greedy. I'd take an ovary, instead. I'd sit with it in my car and call it my girl. I'd point at it with my big hand and stroke it with my small one. Then, at the end, when the time came for us to break up, I wouldn't know where to put my arm. Which direction is the dashboard radio headed; how does this nest want me to break things off? On the last hand, which finger, and after a wide turn, which strange lake?

The Last Days of Leather Production

When the Count's leather factory burnt down the workers found mutilated dogs in the back yard. The dogs had cotton in their mouths, no legs, and bloody openings that had been badly used. That might have been the beginning. Hearing the news, the Count lost his mind, locked himself in the stable and, in an otherworldly voice, began to ask baby Jesus not to bring him more playmates. I understood about the Count, but I couldn't explain everything. The first one I saw was in the bath. It was a girl that had been stuffed, or rather, part of her skin had been stuffed, since she had been a bigger girl. I was about to take a shower, nut. Instead, I nursed this little girl. She was crying because she had gotten lost in the woods. *I'm the forest,* I told her, *and no one lives inside me.* The neighbors listened to everything in that house, the neighbors, and I warned them, but in vain; they did not heed my warnings, though there are more and more people there now. A penguin wrapped in medical gauze with vaginas affixed to its body and a pony made of skin that I called Béla. The job of a good master is not to feed them after midnight, not to be selfish and, if one is cutting his nails, have a taste. I think I'm a good master, but I can't take it much longer. They weren't born like that: someone dug into them and stitched together what they dug up. Their original seeds might still be inside them, somewhere, but the hand is gone. There is no satisfaction in synthetic liner. Where is that hand? The Count couldn't have destroyed it. That would only have been possible if he had eaten it and sewed his mouth shut, but when he gave into his wife's pleas and left the shed, he could still speak. I understand about the Count, but there are still noises in the evening and there is no one who can explain them.

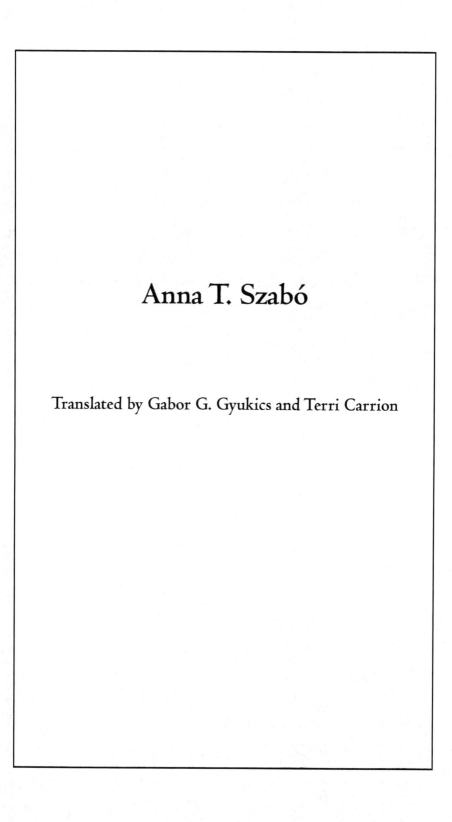

Anna T. Szabó

Translated by Gabor G. Gyukics and Terri Carrion

Ice

Free from the body, that's what I wanted.
My skin is foil, frozen meat inside
To keep it intact for a while.
If I preserve it, it will not spoil.

How great it was to tilt my head back
And feel the bed get burning hot.
The sky is the four walls, gobbles me up,
Makes me one with the other body.

How good it was when another heart
beat inside me, living fire,
the tender fetus I sheltered inside me,
he ate me and from me.

If I don't want this I don't want that either.
If there is no greed, no sin, dead might not exist.
Perhaps conscience, like a mortuary
frees me from corporal decay.

The five senses froze, my soul
frozen inside me. I wasn't free.
Joy completely petrified inside me:
My eternity became my prison.

Leaf

All day you are like a tree in the wind.
You bend with it, but grounded you're pinned.
You want one thing, but don't know what that is.
Until then, you have to stay and wait as is.

In the meantime, let the current twirl you,
make you dance, but don't let it take you.
Free you, but not yet from the corpus,
only from the glimmering surplus.

Later you might understand what remains.
Every device turns visible in the light.
That's the lesson. Too much, too few.
You're complete if you shed your might.

Light Trail

Imagine a pitch-dark room.
How do you know it's a room?
How do you know it's pitch-dark?

Yes, we start walking, stumbling, bump into sharp objects.
But they are not familiar. Spiky, amorphous, hostile terrain.
It is soft now. Squelches like mud. Surrounds and swallows me.

But the eyes are open! Can't see anything.
In operating-room light, in the bright light of day.
Imagine that.

And then: a gap in the shutter.
A needle-point of difference between
Non-light and light.
The inner space throws me out, a heaving hope for
A new start in one tiny point

That you can take
for granted.
Imagine it.

Hawk

I.
Knocking through the night. Breathless.
Unravel. Decode. Dig down.
Sow letters to the wind, heave a word, reap silence.
Silence.

2.
Writing is antilogy. For ourselves, for the rulers.
Hail of knocking. Signs in the snow.
Melted ice. Warmth of machine-gun nest.

Writing is winter talk. Wheel tracks on the
seemingly empty clearing, bloodstain, footprints.
Another story under the snow.

Leaf through the layers.
Moldy book, bones and seeds. The ground,
silent like a grave, tells of everything.

3.
No words on the page, no sentences.
Instead of the winter-book of history
living songs flying up beating,
leafing through the empty space of sky.
There is nothing above it but the sun.
Height. Depth. A single bird is it all.

4.
Then the calligrapher
inhales.
The pen hits the paper the inks starts to scream.

Then he exhales. Steps back.
Silence
again.

Reverse

I realized that flower wasn't going to grow,
its bulb halfway out of the soil
and a few distorted roots swaying.

Dried out, I thought and reached
to lift it out. It was strangely light.
Pulled lengthwise, it didn't want to end—

I watched as from the musky odor,
the hollow depth of the pot,
the glistening, fat white bulb

that I'd planted wrong way up
a perfectly formed hyacinth
emerged with its head down.

An Eye

While you hold the onion with one hand
and cut off the twisted sprout,
an eye looks at you from the center,
a circular iris and greenish pupil,
stare, stare—
then start to cry.

Chase

God creates man,
man creates god,
God becomes man,
man becomes god.
Around-around.
Look in the mirror.
God's eyes stare back at you!

Man ate beast,
beast ate man,
man became beast,
beast became man.
Around-around.
Look in the mirror.
A beast's eyes stare back at you!

God ate beast,
man ate God,
God became beast,
beast became god.
Around-around.
Look in the mirror.
A bloody face stares back at you!

Little Intruder at the Border

Better as a load of meat in a truck
then in wars or in prisons.
Across stormy rivers in a cockleshell,
or tied under the truck's chassis.

Aunt Irene diligently checks
the green border with her binoculars:
My home, my home. Don't take it,
don't even let any foreigners in.

Among a load of meat in the truck
tied under the truck's chassis.
Late night rivers in a cockleshell.
And to camps, to prisons.

Buy It

Let's buy a woman:
She's cheap because she's poor.
Or another one:
She's expensive, because she's rich.
Her virginity. Take it. She'll give it to you.
Or her body. Trust me, a whole novel.

Take her for your wife—Do you have money?—Take her.
Espouse her. Say out loud that she's yours.
Your name will be her name.
Show her off. Beat her.

When you touch her she bleeds or cries.
She pours out words and silence.
In the end she'll freeze into indifference.

Don't get offended. Just pass her on.

Domestic

By God, it's easier with a wild animal.
I'll tell her, but she won't shut her mouth.
I'm telling you, there is no such thing.
Fuck me if I know why she's doing it.

I give her everything she needs.
She has food, yeah! I clothe her. It's beyond her.
What the fuck is so complicated about it?
This ain't a rule: it's a fact. I'm the man.

This Silence

What does this silence want, this silence
scraping me out of the ashes?
What does this call mean?
When did it start?

What does this light want, this light
scraping mefrom beneath the ruin?
Hissing in the center of nothing,
in my tongue,
a burning bush

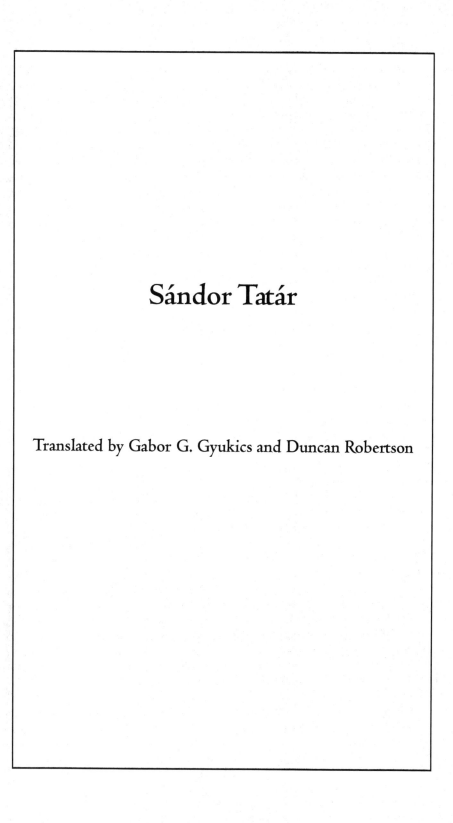

Sándor Tatár

Translated by Gabor G. Gyukics and Duncan Robertson

That's How We Would Give

We leave our loneliness, our anxiety
in a woman's slit. (Sperm always
finds its level.)
We're happy if they accept us in.
But somewhere deep down we know (or realize
sooner or later) that they can't truly unburden us
(not out of wickedness, but simply
because they're not able to).
It stays with us.

And yet.

It's like digging a grave
in the wind. Wide, as Celan
put it. We yearn for something
that would hold us together but wouldn't smother us;
allow us to be ourselves, yet
redeem us from ourselves.
Let her be a hearty plant,
an immovable rock, and the resilient,
warming flesh of an animal too.
Her embrace to suit
our immediate needs.

With less than that, we feel
restless. Though it's a pitifully small thing,
how can we can assuage it:
our loneliness, our anxiety
in a woman's slit...
Afterwards comes (and it's better, better than trying
to change it to words)
our shamefaced and appreciative *coup d'oeil.*

Only If

We don't need to have wine.
but if there are long speeches
let us not grow accustomed to living
in clamor, in excrement.

We must have fire for heat
but if it burns with hungry flames
let the worst of us and their disbelief
be fed to its blaze.

Don't need to have a poem
but if we have one, let it hit hard.
It isn't enough that it chimes and hums
(even a cricket can chirp like a bard!).

Men, don't need to live.
But if they do, let them be happy.
And die after they leave all vain things
too heavy for their souls to carry.

For My Mother

another late lamenting

Did you know, dear mother, who you'd leave behind and for what
when you flagged down the taxi that took you away?
Tell me, did that pang of conscience ever catch up with you?

Or should I have raised myself to be tough,
knowing you did the best you could, realizing—
that the innocent pay for everything.

My days are spent in hiding, drugs put me to sleep:
a burden, a curse is sitting in this languid, rambling shadow.
If it speaks a nice word it certainly lies.
Spell out the unthinkable:
whatever was left of things she was entrusted with, she shattered
(didn't she promise every twentieth...)

I won't whine. It's already too late;
my name is already heavy on the chisel—
as if they'd carve me a tombstone in the first place...
A path awaits, perhaps long as the horizon—
my attention focusing slowly on
a telephone call, what news is coming and when.

That Which Can't be Postponed

The words may move (may ooze) back to you,
when (it might take hours) suffering reaches low tide.
Then they reclaim a few narrow stretches of the beach,
which soon begins to widen; by then they are swarming to return; they do—
romping freely, stretching their limbs, indecent, sunbathing,
mouthing off and flexing their muscles—first a small hill,
then a trench is built, later, a grandiose sandcastle decorated
with seashells and a flag waving proudly on its tallest tower. Enjoy it,
perfect it with devotion; don't worry about anything else
(don't bore yourself with recollections of the past, don't search
         the future)—
the tide comes either way, even if (perhaps) later than first expected,
and then you'll drown.

Prayer for Ignorance

Why comes together what comes together?
And why does it end so pointlessly?
Why is the bathroom an enemy in the morning?
And the moon at night? Why is the table a false promise?

Beyond the window there's a street or a garden
no matter, there is a labyrinth inside you—
your lips would move if they could,
and theology betrays you.

Perhaps it's better not to receive an answer
from those you ask (fate? God?)—
you'll still be asking when there's a hand
on the very last door handle.

Better not to know whether it's your hand
and the handle might not be the one
since you can sense that what you're questioning
is standing at the precipice of pitch-black knowledge.

This is what suits you best: daytime blindness.
Don't tear those divine cotton plugs from your ears,
the wound of your teeth on the apple might yet be healed...

Varietas Delectat

Everything here is the same
purple pulped to grey:
trees, bushes spring wings in spring
and people eat snacks from paper bags.

The hot coffee cooled down to warmish.
Sounds fade in and out over cellphones,
a horsepower parade across the asphalt—
chewing gum turned to sticky lumps.

The squeak of pebbles, tiny feet...
knitting needles clinking,
a swing's howl floods the rooms.
Lights flicker on in the evening.

They're eating cabbage with pasta, rinse the bathtubs
if they're able crawl on each other; this is an
ancient project. Its rhythm moves you,
and those who can't dance...soak their feet.

The garbage truck coughs up the stench.
Teaspoons tinkle on every terrace.
Sober people don't fight the order—
It's all the same here. Always.

The moon measures out silver across poplar branches.
The lake tousles the moon.
Crickets chirp happily.
And the third Parca is getting ready.

My Pictures

There's a crappy feather down in the mud.
It might be pretty,
but what makes things pretty or ugly? Only the brain
is so conceited as to label images of
reality.
That which is spoken without words, the meanings themselves,
and not only their meaning but what lies beyond.
Some of us may reach the mark this way,
some won't,
in accordance with deciphered/misunderstood signs.
Colors toned down through a curtain of rain,
the world seems faded.
Not the rain: Not even a concrete bunker can hide
a thing from anyone who can see.
It could be a star or a melancholy that's been born
inside me—
Either way, I pay rapt attention
but hold my cards close to my chest.
Reality isn't guarded by a bored usher,
but if not this than shouldn't our most
valued possessions be placed under guard?
Isn't there a still more enigmatic painter?
A bungler? An unrecognizable genius?
On the road, from my eyes to my inner self,
(or from my third eye to my hands)
I paint the pictures born
of that place.
They carry messages, loneliness for some, hope for others.
(As if...) Yet the two are one and the same, closer than siblings
at the tit,
God only knows.

János Térey

Translated by Gabor G. Gyukics, Michael Castro,
and Duncan Robertson

In Situ

The street sign shows me the way at midnight.
What a quagmire, oh how brutal!
By Zeus, I'm standing at the corner
of Euripides and Menandros
(thus, in the theater district).

The road cuts a deep turn with no sensible
gradation. Passing indistinct and ugly
row houses, I leap into the darkness:
the kinds of places called forbidden zones.

But everyone is white here. No crescent moons
on cupolas. Slanted stores with shutters
rolled down and locked.
Spare-built shadows thrown out before boozers.
People stop on the corner.
He that approaches wants
to mug me, castrate me, kill me.

A slippery stone sidewalk,
patches on top of patches.
A prostitute watches from under the bent standard of a streetlight.
Its extinguished bulb does not shine on her.

Beyond a shabby fence gapes an empty lot.
A car repair shop or maybe a junkyard,
it acts as a front for a drug dealer.

The buses detour through the park
where not even cops go at night.
Extreme, like a movie scene, this Harlem picture.
Though there aren't any burning oil barrels
or one-eyed beggars.

I'm saying this a zone of pure white
where Athena would decline to vomit.
What would Medea's poet say if he knew
his own street would happily spit in his eye?
Would he be shocked?
Menandros was different. He'd
guffaw with obvious delight.

Only Attica is untouched,
otherwise it's doing fine.
Occasionally, it drinks itself silly, empties itself out,
and *in situ* finds its ancient, creative mood
deadly.

Logistics

I'm your mirror. Your map.
Your car, your chauffeur on top of that.
I call you Champion. Artist.
Even my friend. Don't get me wrong,
I can hear your
thinly-veiled cursing

I'm your cheap Ikea pencil
flicking across the paper, quickening the pace.

I know, there's nothing more boring
and wearisome than someone who
repeats famous names for the sake
of his own sounding better in others' ears.

Like a flea, I jump from one to another.
I post the names of my friends
second to second.
How many gold medals, bronzes, how many catches and pecks,
how many girls in the background...

It's enough to make you puke, right?
Then listen, master:
You can't be seen when my light's off.
You won't make it across the water.
You can't suck your food down without logistics.
They won't eat you if I'm not here to make you look appetizing.
So will you take me with you?

Men Making Peace

Tender or rustic bargaining,
the crushing emotions
of a flag and prisoner exchange:
It'd be great to clear something up... but what?
Spiritual balance, that's the main thing: cathartic peace-making.

Land, wealth, and women interchangeable.
They knock themselves over, grind themselves to pieces,
raze themselves to the ground,
drown themselves in salt,
and later they make peace.
Why and for what?

Man is so often helpless,
like the butterfly in the storm,
though in spirit he takes deadly aim
at New Galaxies.
He makes peace to relax.

Of course, darling, women fight, too.
Wars of great importance. Well, of course!
You think their battles don't
also involve strangers and outer space?

Helen, a *casus belli?* She faded but he survived.
It's the house and the meadow that suffer most.
It's the mothers and wives who suffer
when what happens to men happens
between the zero points of laying down
the axe.

Two Kinds of Darkness

There are two kinds of darkness the merchant knows:
one before opening and one after bankruptcy.

Which one is this? The key to
to selling furniture is a decent window display.
There is silence behind the closed
shutters. Chairs have been set on tabletops.

First risk taken. First fall.
Excitement, first tricks, poker.
Still curious but no one over thirty-five
makes heroic friendships.
Fragile, each new sympathy.

A man understands why business
and not industrial mountaineering.
Why he sits in a glass tower rather than
clambering across the swinging wire.
Sweet dependability!

A beautiful prism but still just architecture.
It's better on the inside. Contemporary art. He talks all
about it. Everything's in bloom, enough of failure.
Suspicion of tax evasion, a flaw in accounting.
                    If you go left I go right,
Like Lot and Abraham. He quietly left his partner.
Has been on his own ever since. The tight years came and he,
who clung so dearly to his goddamn stuff,
learned to let go.

He built his world on inequality.
It wasn't a drive to grab.
He simply gets courageous when
given the chance to compete.

That's the secret, the adrenalin.
And the libido of taking. As a brake
there are a few rules to keep, right?

He cooks. Uncorks the bottle, owns a winery.
Is amused by the adventures of his middle-aged body.
"How do you like it?" he asks, pale with fear.
Digests. He invests what he's saved
in a monolithic golden age.

Announcement

I'd be crazy to settle where famine is the ruler:
I won't have my home on the Porch of Hell.
Should I, a young man, be the officer on duty over there?
To watch over the land in such a dry,
obstinate cold? —Only when the sun goes frozen
I wouldn't be able to leave from there.
I'd be tasting the wine of the region of the Porch of Hell.
There'd be no one to talk to. I'd abuse
the bad wine myself and the walls would have ears.
Someone would hit my stomach, ouch,
sudden, ruthless asault
—"Learn decency, good brother!"—
I'd try to ward off the blows
and my bare hands would grasp the air.

Don't make me have my home on the Porch of Hell—
I prayed before the light turned dark.
In my dream I've got a visitor, my brother, Prince Sure Enough.
Jumping on my chest, he called me three times:

"Old boy, old boy! If you only knew,
what I've been at your age.
I stood among the living smiling.
I've got tenants,I've told them nicely: *You're all mine.*"

"Old boy, you're alone, like my finger.
Previously convicted, and your newest conviction is pestilence.
You've got time, still you ran out.
You're beyond yourself lying in a basement-deep hollow."

"Old boy, I'll get rid of you. I'll take
the food from your mouth and the dream from your mind.
You won't stay on earth anymore.
You'll get ready to move to the Porch of Hell

only when the sun goes frozen, when you'll be crazy.
Last night it was freezing, you weren't out in the street,
you kept yourself awake with me, you righteous fool."

It is bright now. I can no longer see my brother,
Prince Sure Enough. Every sound is familiar, homely.
When a mortal awakens, he is forced to live.
Midday bell tolls, takes me away from home:
I have time to spare and space to walk.

Sorrowful City (exerpt)

The city staggers wearily to its feet
fresh from the new year's depravations.
A great amount of snow falls by morning.
Men lean from mound to mound, stretch
their bodies from one puddle to another
scattered across the blind world.
There's an immense apathy on the roads.
News of parties travels quickly.
Their vibrations make people happy.
In mourning or in failure, they're happy.
What thirst, what urban thirst!
The constant thirst for events,
completely satisfied
by any kind of negative impulse.
Leaden, leaden letters that speak
of gleaming as nourishment in this
bitter weather. The snow is still there on
Tuesday morning. Hasn't been cleared off
by the first day of the New Year.
The snow surprised them, hadn't fallen since
God knows when: a real snow day
in Budapest! The savage citizens wind through
paths carved in the snow between the twelve inch high
embankments. We've had snow since
Advent, but this indeed is something different.

The TV shows a cheerful New Year's concert.
Tick-Tock and *Pizzicato* polkas,
and, of course, *The Blue Danube Waltz*
It does nothing for us, anymore, makes nothing move.

A new calendar? Good. Well, then we
better stuff its virgin pages,
Matrai growls to himself.

For days the New Year mailing was handled by
the machinery of the Ministry of Foreign Affairs,
Pour féliciter nouvel an… Enough of that.
The light of a green-shaded lamp in the bank: that's it.

Matrai producing signs of life through the window
on the first evening of the New Year.
The horse-race, alone, made it tolerable
At Kincsem Park. Dorka, Donner were there
in champagne groove. Tickets in their hands,
they rooted for each other, cheered fanatically
during the last race of the year
for a horse with a pretty name:
Was it Queen of Sheba? Fortune's Son?
Montgomery? Ibiza Sunt? Clarissa?
Scrounging for hot tips
amid the trampling of hooves,
the tension was clearly palpable between them.
Splitting up already…? Could be.
Well, we fumbled the situation,
tied together as we were with scores
of buckles. On and off, we join in on the betting.
My ex hangs off the arm of my friend.
Our elation at the track, our nostalgia,
is mutual. A confrontation is impossible.

He'd forgotten that exhausting graduation
New Year's party on the hill.

… In a rented hotel with a posh raffle
where a few "celebrities" sang evergreen
numbers from old musicals.
A nine-course dinner banquet,
then blistering dances after midnight.
Everyone from the Ministry of Foreign Affairs was there
except Skulteti. It was below him, a different rung.
But not Kovacs, we talked a bit.

Then he simply walked away from me. I don't know
or perhaps know too well...
The lordolatry and the catching rage of becoming
a dignitary carried in every word they uttered,
washed down by tasty oxtail soup.
The well-oiled family ties,
tinkling medals of decorations.
The exception was Binder, that gentleman.
He conjures those magic words:
I'd like to be the ambassador to Lisbon
or Kuala Lumpur, God, honor me,
All of them say it except Binder,
And except weary Matrai.
A few years ago, he was as infected as anybody,
But he's over it now. That's all.
The quiet January evenings are coming.
New Year's Eve is always quiet.

In his dream he made one careless move
and began an avalanche from the eaves of the roof.
Very much like an alpine avalanche,
it ended in mass catastrophe.
Cars with smashed-in hoods buried in snow, and...
He rushed, shivering, down the staircase.
The tenants were gathered around
his mother. He had never seen any of them before.
His quiet little brother came, too.
By that evening—"by the time of your hearing"—
he was being told how to plead in court.
It would be necessary to declare himself not guilty.
Why had this happened under his mother's window?
How had he wound up with snow in his hands? Moreover,
What was he doing up on a roof on Balzac street,
where he had no business being what so ever?
Karanyi had pulled up next to him, slowly rolling down
the window of his Suzuki and said in a mild,
cynical way, *So, I've heard, I've heard...*

After all, nothing matters to a kibitzer.

He woke at noon sharp with a lingering headache.
The bell. His mother had arrived unannounced and was ringing the bell.
How strange. "Say, what's up?"
She took a step closer to her son.
"Is Blanka your lover? Your own cousin…?
Son, it's awful. I won't believe it."
"How'd you find out?" "It's practically an open
secret. Julia let it slip. My sweet boy,
I'm dumbfounded. You two playing footsy together?
This, I—" She stared. Licked her lips.
"Your cleaning lady is busy?"
She wasn't just staring, she was surveying the flat
like a police detective taking stock of his surroundings.
She began pacing in circles. "You came to
check on me? What are you looking for?" "Nothing, dear."
An awful woman, thinks Matrai.
She decides to be dishonest.
She chooses to be pushy! Too bad.
She, my mother plays the part so convincingly.
Vera walked around, touching the shelves, and
since she was unable to find anything, got ready to leave.
Quickly, she peeked into the bathroom.
"No clean laundry for New Year's Day?!"
"Come on. Are you serious, that's what bothers you?"
"Hey, it's just an old superstition." Matrai was shocked
to see his mother light a cigarette.
"Do that on the balcony, please. Well, it's over anyway.
We broke up last year." His mother was staring at him,
not knowing whether to believe him,
She squinted her eyes
Then left without saying good bye.

Is this how they'll all leave me in the end?
Matrai let his head loll back and forth a few times.
Unhurriedly, he turned up the heater.

He lit a candle, which he seldom did. Inhaled
the rich sandalwood aroma of the incense,
dusting all the while. Contemplating.
No, it wasn't Blanka. It was Fruzsina he was interested in.
The stenographer. She wasn't being looked after.
I must admit that Fruzsina has also disappeared.
But who hasn't? Everyone was gone
by the time needles began nicely dropping
from the pines.
Thousands of dreams lie resting like oysters
on beds of ice. Was it all in vain?
Iron times. The time of great remorse.
An elusive time of hopes bound up
in bowls of lentil soup. It is the time of the filet of perch.
Time for leftovers. Time for heartburn: Hydrochloric acid.
At present, Budapest sits on an Eastern death row,
a humiliated and ragged city in crisis
during an extraordinary winter.
Men work on the levees,
on platforms in the tube, in blue buses,
and in pizzerias with absolutely no vibe.
A fine dusting of powder sits atop
last year's snowdrifts. Bad mood.
New Year's Eve is quiet and dead.

Later, at the fifth reception at the Swedish
Embassy, a place with a deficit of good cheer, the room
is only half full. Budapest is staggering,
recovering gradually. The roofs are heavy
with packed snow. The corporation is being represented
by Vendelin, the kindly Czech ambassador.
"*Co je nového*," he asks gently.
"*Nic zvlástniho*," answers Matrai,
scanning Vendelin's wide face.
The balancing of foreigners requires
elaboration and it's difficult to accomplish.
He takes a clumsy step back. Yet Vendelin

notices something in Matrai,
uncertainty, at the very least:
I've never noticed before. The man is insecure. -
"The Circle would be so boring without you,"
says Vendelin with a wide smile.
"You had better things to do?" "Someone else handled it this year."
"But who?" "Well, the President's man."
"Last year you were there too." "I helped."
"It was boring without you." A New Year! Waking up early
to watch his zealous president march
before a line of ambassadors,
receiving the best wishes of each.
And they make their introductions one by one:
"A conveyor belt. That he was no longer part of this,
was an unexpected relief."

Then came the disillusive melting of snow.
Plus, Blanka wrote another letter.
She feels sorry for what happened.
Coquettishly mentions Evelin…
"How was Hannukah?" *Was that casual antisemitism?*
I might take it that way out of malice.
Oh, this is only a crumb of penance
wrapped in cellophane. I don't know, not enough.
Another film rolling in my mind,
thinks Matrai with resignation.
Csúcs Hill, way above the snow-line!
By the time I learned the way to her place,
the walk up there, it was time to forget it.
No. It won't get any better—a resounding no.
And Matrai expunges this dribble of a confession:
Got to keep moving and not laterally.
He has lunch with his mother, only salad.
"What was it, you were looking for
At my place?" "You know, signs of Blanka."
Matrai looks his mother dead in the eye,
hand wobbling over the keys of the

piano. Schubert. He stops,
watching Vera's wide pupils.
He takes a slim case out of his pocket:
"God bless you, it's your name day tomorrow."
"Ágoston, how nice: as if you didn't know…
I thought you'd forgotten." "Me?"
Matrai laughs wryly.
He says goodbye and takes a stroll through the city.
At Theatre Víg he takes a look at the program,
and he stumbles into something on the steps.
Look, a dead pigeon … like packed snow.
The tip of his shoe barely nudges it.

Krisztina Tóth

Translated by Gabor G. Gyukics and Terri Carrion

Tourist

I've just arrived in the city where
you didn't come with me. Everyone was heading home:
close-faced women, neatly-combed men.
It was writen all over me that I was a dead tired
stranger.
There was a double bed,
but only one candy on the pillow.
The safe was pointed out to me
right at the reception desk.
I was wondering what I could put inside
that I would leave here as a souvenir, something
that's accessible, expensive,
and after, I need to figure out how to live,
to forget the code
as soon as possible.

The city where you didn't come with me
was cooler than at home. I wandered along
windy streets looking for the display.
I had an hour among the shelves of a
Chinese store, The clerk watched me
cagily from behind the counter.
It was writen all over me that I was a dead tired
stranger.
"How fragile we are,"
mumbled Sting on the radio.
I paid, searching for change.
The robot that survived the luggage rack
broke at the very moment I got home.
It started spinning, fell backwards
on the carpet and stared as if
—as my son said about the battery—
its heart had been taken out.

Still, when you came, it never went well.
And in the second city, a sore grew on your lips
during the night.
We couldn't remember the word *herpes* in English,
so you puckered your lips, pointed at them in the pharmacy,
leaned over the counter like a Romeo.
The woman in the coat finally understood
and served us with disgust.

In the third city the toilet clogged.
We stared at it. It was packed with shit
like under the tail of a skulking animal.
When flushing, the animal clattered,
so we didn't dare irritate it again.
The Portugese plumber asked us where
we were from, probably pondering
whether we had flush toilets, and
flapper-flush valves and things like that.
You can't feel you're being detested or taken,
you said in bed that night. We talked
about repairmen instead of making love.

The city where you didn't come with me,
I walked through fast. Fancy clock in the main square
measured the time it had spent with me.
A man with a laptop stared at me
for a long time in the hotel elevator,
the scent of morning aftershave lingering around him.
I could love anyone but you I thought.
We'd walk, he holding the umbrella clumsily.
I'd lie to him, saying you had called.
In fact, they'd send me the bill.
I ran out of everything. I had reasons for one.
My too-loose clothes were hanging on me, my life.
It was writen all over me that I was a dead tired
stranger.
I pushed the wrong button on the coffee maker,

I recoiled as steam shot out.
There wasn't one clean table to be found.

The city where you didn't come with me,
was sowed with rain. It took me three years
to return.
Since then the rain had ripened:
I reached the store by cutting a path
with an umbrella through gauzy stems.
Their stock hasn't changed much.
I've purchased a purse. I threw the old one,
which you knew, into a dumpster in the parking lot
next to the hotel. No one saw it, but I still felt
like a pickpocket who robbed someone,
one who is not even in this poem, a grifter
who took off with her trolley case leaving
her unpaid past behind.

The city where you didn't come with me,
I remember as a place of lacking.
How many places I've been without you since.
After all, I have you to thank for me becoming a
professional tourist. I cross from one year
to another, never forgetting that you must go
home from every place you've been to.
Until then
I can manage with a good map,
go anywhere on sleepless nights,
wander dense alleys of recollection as
the continent of a previous life enters my mind,
where on a bathroom sink where, with toothpaste dried
into its white bristles, your stupid electric toothbrush
faces the tile like an old, offended punk.

Talking

1.

I'm always talking in your dreams,
but not in a human tongue. My voice is different,
but you recognize it nonetheless,
just like you see my face in so many creatures.
It's impossible to climb through the clay-like mud
of the autumn hillside, but there might be a path
that will take us back to summer.
Your eyes are closed so you need to stand there.
Watch out, don't step on the black snails.
They draw a map with their crawling trails,
I hope the flood of days won't wash it away.
How else will you come back?

2.

Lost, wet dogs arrive at night,
walk around the house.
Outside, great dripping thujas stand in line
and sway back and forth like ghosts.
I can hear almost everyone sneaking in.
Humans, animals who went far away
step into my dream to hold my hand.
From their breaths, I create a patchwork face
of the one who stood up and let it go.
Earth has a scent after the rain.
Listening, I hear you shake your head.
You'll knock and I won't mistake you for the rain.

Blind Map

For my son

Slithering strata, faces of mountain ranges,
subliminal Mariana Trench, magma in the soul, what for

what are the slant woods, the migrating crows,
the erratic rivers for, they live, die out,
penguins on ice floes,

what for
the swimming clouds of torn DNA chains,
the closed eyes of the currents in the water
if it cannot find

a course, it's dragging its constantly sad route
and whereever he reaches it's a war,
death plows a gutter,

the world doesn't need to be
jumbled up with names,
birth and love spasmodic screams:

cities, ventriloqial fate,
corrie of remembrance, living
lines, see

how all circle and none has a route,
it's always the mothers who give birth to orphancy
always

The Lover's Dream

I applied to become a castle guard, the people in his house were pretty,
like himself: his children were blond and tall.
The house lay on a hillside at the end of a shaded street.
They waved in front the fence, waiting.

Their dog used belong to me. I brought a drawing
showing them how the dog once looked.
We loved each other. Planned for all of us
to live together in tea-color quietude.

The blind wife scrubbed the white stairs.
He pointed at her saying, *My wife.*
The way he leaned down to her showed his tenderness.
I was waiting for him to walk me up to the attic.

When I lived with them, I carried parasols to the garden,
that was my job and to watch over their children,
while I loved him day night beyond measure
walking up and down the white stairs.

Then, one day came the storm. I carried the toys
and pillows inside from the garden terrace
and like someone looking up from a blank book,
I realized suddenly that it was all to no avail.

So, I cut their heads off and placed them in washed-out jars
carefully, all facing forward on the edges of the
marble staircase paying attention not to spill
their blood onto the stone.

I cried too, I think, but I knew I wasn't insane,
that it was his stare that turned the screw, and it hurt
        that I could never again see his gaudy, sweat-spangled forehead
glorified by procreation.

They'll Be Good for Seed

My dad ill with cancer
angrily weeds in the garden
leaning over his huge belly
he sits on the cutty stool pulling
thick black roots out of the greasy soil

My dad ill with cancer
wanders sleepless in the house.
Goes to the kitchen, looks around,
knocks things over, turns the lights on and off
crushes a sleeping spider.

My dad ill with cancer
can't eat anything anymore.
Places two wafers on the plate,
falls back, plays with the remote,
watches cooking shows.

My dad ill with cancer
thinks of old swimming pools.
I talk to him, he looks away.
The rhythm is important, he mumbles, to have a good stroke,
like Katinka Hosszú.

My dad ill with cancer,
the freckles on his arm are swollen.
The same hand I was scared of.
He puts a teaspoon next to my coffee
with three cubes of sugar.

My dad ill with cancer
cleans the drawer.
Packs the medicines,
figuring out how many he took,
what needs to be prescribed.

My dad ill with cancer
settles next to the flowerbed,
jiggles their dry little heads,
They'll be good for seed, shows me his palm.
Take these and scatter them in the fall.

Dog

It seemed like a lump of black earth
or a heap of snow fallen from the hillside
during the thaw. It started to darken.
Only the sleeting earth was visible in the landscape,
the windows covered with steam,
and as we got closer, it seemed
to move, like a coat lifting up its arms,
a shadow hitchhiker thrown to the roadside
and run over by the headlights' gaze.

It appeared to appear then disappear,
but as every car in the lane went around it,
I started to watch the curb to see what it was.
Suddenly it appeared, like a sinking body.
His front feet were braced in the mud as if to stand,
its nose up to the wind, his upper body watching.
But behind it I saw his hindquarter was shattered to pulp,
the bones of his back legs poking out of the bloody hair.
As the half-dog steadily jerked, mouth open,
I saw in his eyes that he saw everything.

I screamed, *Stop the car, pull over.* I begged you
to save it, run it over it, someone behind
us should hit it. But what should be done?!
What should be done?—you raised your voice,
What do you want from me?!
Tell me, what do you want from me?
I wanted you to stop, get it in the car or kill it.
The dog was there between us that whole week.
It will be better at home, we thought,
but it felt as if we'd pushed it into the street
and then always went around it with words.

Still I couldn't not want you to lean over me
that evening: I stared at your tight arms,
tried not to think about that body,
the way it leaned at the edge of the ditch,
its rhythmic movements while your eyes
stared into the distance without saying a word.
How much, how much furious regret is in your
lovemaking, the way you asked, *What do you want from me?*
while hitting the steering wheel. You're not even looking at me
and behind your shoulder a blood-soaked
winter sky becomes visible through the drizzling rain.

Sunday

"Those would be good," my mother pointed at
the socks with the word Sunday on them.
"We need at least ten pair, I gotta run," she gasped.
"It's noon already, my husband can't eat, sleeps
and waits, his legs as cold as if he were dead.
I prepared some meat soup for dinner."

"Good socks," said the Chinaman.
A fallen tower lay, just lay there while
a patient, stiff-winged butterfly sat on
its paper-petal-thin veins.
"Good socks." The face of the merchant shone
as he licked open the striped plastic bag.

I said nothing, of course, about the thing
bleeding tar, the decomposing tissue,
the sagging sutures. "Good socks,"
he nodded and started to empty the fallen-over sack.
The socks stayed in the hospital.
I have no idea what day that was.

My inheritance is a bag of rag balls.
Dad, do you remember that shining moment
at the fair, at the shooting gallery
when I hit the target and you touched my shoulders?
Whispered to me, holding rag balls in your hand,
to show them that it wasn't an accident.

Since then I've started to practice with
new rag balls. Maybe one day I'll
hit the target again. You watch me
from above as I spoil every throw,
Sunday, Sunday and that autumn fair.
It gets dark early, and I'm fairly cold.

Song of a Secret Life

My secret life's a cat gliding among parked cars,
a shadow on the firewall, memory torn at its heel.

My secret life's lived in your wakeful eyes,
completely close your scratched eyes on me.

My secret life's an empty room echoing in my head,
once leaning out of its window I sang dark songs.

My secret life's a pigeon carcass reeking on a rundown roof,
faded clothes against the sky, death will grow in it one day.

My secret life's a crack running beyond a living face,
a road beyond time in a place where I'm not angry yet.

My secret life's a station that trains race through,
by the time I count to ten, it'll be silence and darkness.

My secret life's a few scanned moments,
wrinkled pages torn from a lost notebook.

My secret life's incomplete, forever baffling,
it collates my fading face together.

My secret life's a yellow embankment full of garbage,
desire traveling inside a body and time spent in earthy places.

My secret life's been slammed shut and became a secret,
at dawn, the dream is banging at the door.

My secret life's what you see passing by,
completely close your scratched eyes on me.

My secret life's been invented to live through,
its light is on in that far away house.

Szabina Ughy

Translated by Gabor G. Gyukics and Terri Carrion

New Homeland

You're on the road again,
lead by the invisible prints of beauty.
Everything falls toward the horizon,
whatever was gathers there.
Your mother brought you from the source
of the waves, since then you've been eaten
by the disease of return.
You can't see anything
you haven't seen before:
abandoned paths in the woods,
the skies that separate days and seasons,
the shape of flying flocks of birds,
orange groves, rain and sea
all say
they aren't visible for themselves.
Nothing is gone, only walking,
sensitive as the soles of your feet
as you mark the borders of your new homeland with your steps.

Mist

Laying in a tub full of water is like
slipping back to my mother.
The drain's chain wraps around the toe,
hair around the thighs.
The wrinkled skin of the palm
swallows faith.
If I rub the scab with the sponge,
it might come off like a temporary
chewing gum tattoo at Lake Balaton.
But the cancer tattoo doesn't wear off.
The body doesn't forget.
I place my head on the rim of the tub,
draw my message to God in the mist.

For the Joy of Wind

Days came and went.
Homeless mornings,
goodness all over.
The tension of sight hurts
like the shadow hurts the light.
The recognition was simply
like the line of the horizon
or the whiteness of seagulls.
I've turned into a stranger while
traveling through existence.
I had a companion
only when the wind rose.
I stood inside
to get to know it,
I walked inside
to give myself to it,
and to fill it with delight,
I ran with it.

Pier

It starts raining in the morning,
water falls on water,
the harbor lights brighten up.

Sailing a bit closer, the writing shows:
"You'll leave, come back, and never die."

His foot trembles on the batten as he reaches land
and the safety of something slow and heavy
begins to pulsate in him.

He collects sunshine, strength, and burden.
One can live a life like that,
madness slowly rationed is mercy.

He decides which century he lives in
yet the bell tolls every quarter hour
reminding him of how to measure his life.

He holds on to the afternoons,
uses them to watch
how the flesh of time
crushes itself on the concrete of the pier.

But as the street sucks up
his body on foggy evenings
he feels a throbbing absence
in his bones again and again.

How much of everything could be still?

An angel resides in certain assents,
the angel of sudden decision.
Behind it wide light of direction gleams on
the face of the dark bay, drifting away the scar of silence.

Foldout

There's an island in the south sea,
its sweet flesh a dark abundant mound.
There's a city, the time inside it
denser than honey flare.
There's an unfinished church,
a glassy cupola made of prayer.
There are things that were born distorted.
There are doves that break the immovable
lines of the square with their flight.
There are black streets and benches
where you sit as it turns to Sunday,
and there are squares where all these
things won't happen to you.
There are balconies that are good only for smoking.
There are faces with stories
that need to be hidden like severed limbs.
There are children who work late hours,
their laughter grows like shadows on the wall.
There are pretty woman that when you look in their eyes
icy ribbons spring from your fingertips.

Rest Mass

The walls are sore muscles,
the wet concrete the shells of turtles,
shining in the night.

Boats sunbathe on the black oil-slick water
of the Danube, each are the bequest
of a transparent God.

That woman in the square under the blanket
tore a flashing sliver
from a loaf of bread
with both hands
suggesting
that everyone should have
a statue
made of reminiscence,
white marble,
glass and light,
that everyone should have
at least one
impeccable life
somewhere
that would pose as a model
of wholeness
since the beginning of time.

For the stars and bodies
to become one
the denial of distance is needed.

Beyond

We slowly poison each river,
city-size islands of trash float in the oceans
but don't worry, there are
endless spaces open to destruction.
I say *to destruction*, but I could rephrase it
as above, under, next to, around.
I wouldn't be entirely correct,
but this way it could well be imagined
and the memory of memories is an approach
toward the home lying beyond the letters,
the torsos of each word we utter.
Lean on the verb, the wall, stretch against the wind,
beyond bone and concrete, beyond the city,
beyond beyond, what an impossible word it is.
Beyond your actions
your body's outline is
like the thousand-times touched curve
of a staircase's railing
subtly glistening.

In One Place

Perhaps I shouldn't move at all,
but sit in one place
a burning presence,
fly to the sky,
endure pain quietly,
let silence
reduce our questions to ashes.
Everything that's alive is aflame,
as if it wants to perish.

Fata Morgana

I thought I was late
but then my host warned me
not to say the word *late* anymore.
This is the only forbidden word on the island.
By using it we might disturb
the spawning of the fish swimming in the coastal waters.
There is no future or past tense only past perfect in their language.
They don't identify themselves with their actions.
One can't get familiar with the inhabitants through their burial customs,
their teeth or the progress of their weaponry.
So how can we get to know them, I've asked after a long silence.
This island shows one face to those
who come from the sea
and another to those who come from land.
It shows a different face to children
and another to those who live among its memories.
Many sailed by without noticing the island,
their minds covered by *Fata Morgana*, the mist of disbelief.
The nearby seaport is drawn in the distance
but in that distance becomes distorted and unreal.
Where am I, I've asked, screaming.
As an answer he pointed at a poster:
This island is not reflecting itself.
The sky is its mirror. Only when you see
the white ranges of its mountains,
the constellation of its cities,
or the pattern on a blade of bent grass
will that be true distance.

Justifiction

We are searching for Him in everything.
Something we assume,
are ashamed to admit.

Seeing in not seeing.
Hearing in not hearing.
Knowing in not knowing.
Following the course of the river.

Everyone goes toward silence,
wanting to be a sea.

The Contributors

János Áfra (b. 1987 in Hajdúböszörmény) currently lives in Debrecen. He studied visual arts, literature, and philosophy at the University of Debrecen, where he is presently an instructor. He has published three books of poetry: *Glaukóma (Glaucoma)* in 2012, *Két akarat (Two Wills)* in 2015, and *Rítus (Ritual)* in 2017. Áfra was awarded two Hungarian debut prizes as well as several other awards. He also authored a play which premiered in 2014. Editor-in-chief of KULTer.hu and editor of *Alföld* literary magazine, he also writes essays and art criticism.

Johanna Domokos (b. 1970 in Sovata, Romania) is a poet, translator, literary scholar, theorist. Recipient of the Faludy prize, she is an associate professor at the Károli Gáspár University and the director of the Literary Translator's Laboratory Gruppe Bie at Bielfiled University, Germany. She studied Hungarology, Finno-Ugristics and Semiotics at the University of Cluj, Szeged and at TU Berlin. Her research focuses on the translation and analysis of multicultural literature in Scandinavia (particularly Sami and Finnish). In addition to two monographs and numerous scientific articles, she has published seventeen literary translations from Finnish, Sámi and English into Hungarian and twelve books of her own literary work.

Gabor G. Gyukics (b. 1958) is a jazz poet and literary translator. Born in Budapest, he is the author of eleven books of original poetry. He has published six in Hungarian, two in English, one in Arabic, one in Bulgarian, and one in Czech. His sixteen books of translation include *A Transparent Lion: Selected Poetry of Attila József* and *Swimming in the Ground: Contemporary Hungarian Poetry* (in English, both with co-translator Michael Castro) and an anthology of North American Indigenous poets in Hungarian titled *Medvefelhő a város felett*. His latest book in English, *a hermit has no plural*, was published by Singing Bone Press in 2015. His latest book in Hungarian was published by Lector Press in 2018. He received the Füst Milan translator's prize in 1999 and 2017. Thanks to a CEC Arts Link grant, he was able to establish the first Open Mike and Jazz Poetry reading series in Hungary in 2000. In September 2020, he received the Hungary Beat Poet Laureate Lifetime Award from the National Beat Poetry Foundation USA.

Attila Jász (b. 1966 in Szany) is a poet and essayist and author of thirteen books of original poetry. The winner of several literary prizes, including the prestigious József Attila prize, he is chief editor of Új Forrás Publishing and its literary magazine. His latest collection, *Inside Angel,* was published by Kortárs Press in 2019.

Dénes Krusovszky (b. 1982 in Debrecen) is a poet, editor,and translator. He is the author of five books of original poetry, one children's book, one book of short stories, a book of essays, and a novel. In addition he has translated three collections of literature and has been awarded the József Attila prize, among many other prestigious awards. He is the founding editor of *versumonline.hu* online magazine.

Gábor Lanczkor (b.1981 in Székesfehérvár) is a poet, writer, and translator. He completed his studies in Budapest and has spent long periods in Rome, Ljubljana, and London. He is an award-winning author with fifteen published books: novels, poetry, children's literature and essays. He was guitarist in the band Médeia Fiai and is involved in the musical projects Anarchitecture and Los Reyes Católicos. His selected poems in English was published under the title *Sound Odyssey* in 2016. He is chief editor of *1749.hu* online magazine.

Júlia Lázár (b. 1960 in Budapest) is a poet, translator, and educator. She has published four volumes of poetry, *Fingerprints* (1988), *Unknown* (2001), *Still* (2011), and *Stoneface* (2016), as well as numerous translations of prose and poetry from English. Authors she has translated include Oscar Wilde, Robert Graves, W. B. Yeats, Walt Whitman, E.M. Forster, George Orwell, Sylvia Plath, and Ted Hughes.

Mónika Mesterházi (b. 1967 in Budapest), a poet, essayist, and freelance literary translator has published four books of poetry (1992, 1995, 1999, 2007) and, in 2019, a book of essays on 20th century and contemporary Hungarian poetry. She has received awards for both her poetry and translations, including the prestigious József Attila prize. Her poems appeared in Swedish in *Två ungerska poeter,* (2009). English translations were published in the anthologies: *In Quest of the Miracle Stag: The Poetry of Hungary* Vol. II, ed. by Ádám Makkai (1997); *An Island of Sound: Hungarian Poetry and Fiction Before and Beyond the Iron Curtain* (2004); *New Order: Hungarian Poets of the Post 1989 Generation,* ed. by George Szirtes (2010), and in the Hungarian issue of *Modern Poetry in Translation* (2018).

Zita Murányi (b. 1982 in Budapest) is a poet, writer, and journalist. Author of two books of original poetry and two novels, she received the Bródy Sándor prize for her first book of prose in 2004. She is also the recipient of the Móricz Zsigmond prize for young writers.

Zsuka Nagy (b. 1977 in Nyíregyháza) is a poet, writer, teacher, and author of four collections of poetry. She lives and works as a teacher in Nyíregyháza. She likes poetic images just as she likes riding the bycicle she calls Rozi. She has received several prestigious awards for her work

Márió Z. Nemes (b. 1982 in Ajka) is a poet, editor, and essayist. Author of three books of original poetry and two essay collections, he has received several literary prizes for young authors.

Anna T. Szabó (b. 1972 in Kolozsvár, Romania) is a poet and translator. She is the author of twenty-two books of original poetry and two books of prose. She has translated seventy-six children's books from English, including those by Beatrix Potter and Dr. Seuss. She is the winner of numerous literary prizes, including the prestigious József Attila prize.

Sándor Tatár, Ph.D. (b. 1962 in Budapest), a poet and translator of German literature, is a librarian at the Hungarian Academy of Science. He is the author of five books of original poetry including four in Hungarian and one in a bilingual edition: *Bejáró m vész* (2007)and *a magyar–német: A végesség kesernyés v… / Endlichkeit mit bittrem Trost* (2006). He is the recipient of the Salvatore Quasimodo and the prestigious József Attila prizes. Together with German poet Paul Alfred Kleinert, he received the Alfred Müller-Felsenburg prize.

János Térey (1970–2019), a poet, writer, playwright, and translator, was born in Debrecen. He authored ten books of original poetry, eight books of prose, and four plays in verse. He was the winner of numerous prizes, including the prestigious József Attila prize. He is considered one of the greatest Hungarian poets of the Twenty-first Century. In 2020, the Petőfi Literary Museum launched a scholarship for middle generation writers, poets, and translators in his name.

Krisztina Tóth (b. 1967 in Budapest) is poet, writer, translator, and glass artist. Author of thirteen books of original poetry, she is one of the most highly acclaimed contemporary Hungarian writers and the winner of awards including the Graves Prize (1996), Déry Tibor Prize (1996), József Attila Prize (2000). She was Hungary's Poet Laureate in 2008, one of the highest honors in Hungarian literature. Her poems have a subtle combination of strong visual elements, intellectual reflection and a very empathic, yet often ironic concern with everyday scenes, conflicts and people. A women writer engaged in the poetics of body, her work is considered by many of her interpreters as "ecriture femmine." Since her first collection of short stories was published in 2006, she has been listed among the best contemporary writers of Central Europe. Her poetry and prose have been translated to more than fifteen languages.

Szabina Ughy (b. 1985 in Ajka) is a bibliotherapist and poet who also writes fairytales. She has authored two books of original poetry, *Külső protézis* (2011), and *Séták peremvidéken* (2015) and novel titled *A gránátalma íze* (2018).

Michael Castro (1945-2018) was a native of New York City who lived in St. Louis for most of his adult life. He was a poet and translator. He published ten collections of his own poetry, most recently *We Need to Talk: New & Selected Poems*, as well as the literary history, *Interpreting the Indian: Twentieth Century Poets and the Native American.* Castro was the co-founder of River Styx, a community-based literary organization that has produced *River Styx* magazine and readings in St. Louis since 1975, as well as his long-running radio program, Poetry Beat. He frequently performed his work, often in collaboration with musicians, all over the United States, in England, Hungary, Scotland, Senegal, and India. He received the Guardian Angel of St. Louis Poetry Award from River Styx (2000) and the Warrior Poet Award from *Word in Motion* (2005). In 2015 Castro was named St. Louis's first Poet Laureate.

Michael Castro and Gabor Gyukics were long-time collaborators in rendering Hungarian poetry into American English. The titles they translated together are:
My God, How Many Mistakes I've Made, Selected Poetry of Endre Kukorelly. (2015)
Terrenum, a book of poetry and art by visual artist Ádám Gáll. (2009)
A Transparent Lion, Selected Poetry of Attila József. (2006)
Gypsy Drill: Collected Poetry of Attila Balogh. (2006)
Consciousness by Attila József. (2005)
Swimming in the Ground: Contemporary Hungarian Poetry (2002)

Terri Carrion was conceived in Venezuela and born in New York to a Galician mother and Cuban father. Her work has appeared and disappeared in print and online. She is co-founder of the global grassroots movement 100 Thousand Poets for Change.

Jan Garden Castro's books include *The Last Frontier* (poetry, Eclectic Press), *The Art and Life of Georgia O'Keeffe*, and *Sonia Delaunay: La Moderne*. She's contributing editor for *Sculpture Magazine*, and co-editor of *Margaret Atwood: Vision and Forms*. She received the CCLM Editor's Award for *River Styx Magazine*, an award from the Camargo Foundation and two NEH Fellowships. She's curated exhibitions in Japan, Peru, and the U.S.A., and is acting head of PEN Women. See www.jancastro.com/.

Duncan Robertson is a writer from Seattle, WA. He earned his B.A. in English at Lewis and Clark College and is a founding editor of *Panel* magazine. He has written for CYD Films, and currently splits his time between Budapest and Prague.

Tom Stolmar was born in Detroit in 1961. After living in Düsseldorf, Germany, he went to live in San Francisco where he became a member of the notorious Barbarians of the Post-Beat Generation. He earned his B.A. in poetics at The New College of California. He has published three books of poetry and is presently working on a novel.

Belinda Subraman has been writing poetry since the sixth grade and publishing since college. She had a ten-year run editing and publishing *Gypsy Literary Magazine* and edited *Henry Miller and My Big Sur Days* by Judson Crews for Vergin Press. She also published the Sanctuary Tape Series, which was a remastered compilation of audio poetry and original music from around the world. She has a Master of Arts degree from California State University. Her archives are housed at University of New Mexico, Albuquerque. Her most recent book is *Left Hand Dharma* (Unlikely Books, 2018).

Notes on the Poems

Page 62:
Miklós Perényi is a well-known Hungarian cellist.

Page 64: Kapolcs is a tiny village of just 442 people in Hungary.

Page 77:
František Rint was a 19th-century Czech woodcarver and carpenter. In 1870, he was employed by the House of Schwarzenberg to organize the human bones interred at the Sedlec Ossuary, a small Christian chapel in Sedlec. Rint began to make things—baroque, fantastical and unlikely—from the bones, and ultumately decorated the entire chapel with bones.

Page 89:
Gaeta is on the coast of central Italy, between Rome and Naples.

Michelangelo Merisi da Caravaggio was an Italian painter active in Rome for most of his artistic life. Born September 29, 1571, in Milan, he died on July 18, 1610, in Porto Ercole.

Page 90:
Percy Bysshe Shelley drowned, along with two other men, when his large boat capsized and sank off the coast of Pisa, Italy. The bodies washed ashore eight days later on the beach near Viareggio and were temporarily interred. Quarantine laws made it necessary for the bodies of the drowned to be burned. Edward Trelawny, a friend of both Byron and Shelley and the designer of the boat on which Shelley died, ordered the construction of a "furnace of iron" on the beach, after which the bodies were dug up and prepared for cremation. Lord Byron wanted to cut out and keep Shelley's heart but was not permitted to do so. A crowd, including Lord Byron, gathered on the beach to witness the cremation. Byron, overcome with emotion, stripped off his clothes and swam out to sea. After the cremation, it was alleged that Shelley's heart had survived the fire.

Page 92:
Hegyestu is an 8 million year old volcanic outcropping that has been quarried. Apparently most of the basalt cobblestone in cities like Budapest originates from here.

Ság and Badacsony are volcanoes in Western Hungary. Between 3-6 million years old, they have been extensively mined for basalt.

Page 100:
Ophelia is a character in William Shakespeare's drama *Hamlet*. She is a young noblewoman of Denmark and potential wife of Prince Hamlet, who, due to Hamlet's actions, ends up in a state of madness that ultimately leads to her drowning.

Page 106:
Prospero is the protagonist of William Shakespeare's play *The Tempest*. He has learned sorcery from books, and uses it while on the island to protect Miranda and control the other characters.

Caliban is also a character in *The Tempest*. Shakespeare described him as in contact with the pure and original forms of nature; the character grows out of the soil where it is rooted, uncontrolled, uncouth, and wild.

Page 114:
Havlíček Gardens is a park in Prague that was inspired by the Italian Rennaisance.

Stromvoka is considered to be Prague's Central Park and is also a Royal Game Preserve.

Page 122:
Csepel Island, the largest island in Hungary, is located in the Danube River

Page 132: A Csepel camping bicycle is a small bicycle designed to be easy to take on a camping trip.

Page 134:
French poet François Villon (1431–1463) was known to be a criminal.

Page 137:
A Puli is a small Hungarian herding dog with a coat that looks like dreadlocks.
Nyet kupit is Russian and means *Do not buy.*

Page 144:
The title is a reference to *The Breasts of Terésias*, a play by French poet and play-wright Guillaume Apollinaire. (1880–1918). In the subtitle *Drame surréaliste*, as well as in the preface to the play, the poet invented the word *surrealism* to describe his new style of drama. The play tells the story of Thérèse, who changes her sex to obtain power among men, with the aim of changing customs, subverting the past, and establishing equality between the sexes.

Alexander Pushkin (1799 – 1837) was a Russian poet, playwright, and novelist of the Romantic era. His novel-in-verse, *Eugene Onegin*, deals with the relationship between fiction and real life and the deadly inhumanity of social convention.

Page 147:
Antoine Marie Joseph Paul Artaud, better known as Antonin Artaud (1896–1948), was a French dramatist, poet, essayist, actor, and theatre director, widely recognized as one of the major figures of twentieth-century theater and the European avant-garde and known for his raw, surreal and transgressive themes.

Page 149:
In 2019, Pope Francis visited His Holiness Bartholomew I, Archbishop of Constantinople, after sending him a gift of relics of St. Peter meant to be placed next to the relics of Apostle Andrew, who is venerated as the heavenly patron of the Church of Constantinople, as confirmation of the journey that their two churches had made in drawing closer to one another.

Page 150:
An industrial accident at a caustic waste reservoir took place at a bauxite plant in western Hungary in October 2010. The environmental disaster left 2.5 million people temporarily without safe drinking water. The toxic waste—with cyanide levels 400 times the maximum normal amount — poured into local rivers, ultimately inflicting serious damage on more than 1,000 kilome-

ters of waterway in the Danube ecosystem in four countries.

Page 163:
A cockleshell is a light, flimsy boat.

Page 166:
"Another late lamenting" refers to the title of a poem by Attila József (1905–1937), "Late Lamenting." The poem appears in *A Transparent Lion*, translated by Michael Castro and Gabor G.Gyukics and published by Green Integer Press in 2006.

Page 168:
Coup d'oeil translates roughly as *glance* or *glimpse*.

Page 173:
Varietas delectat means *Variety is the spice of life*.

The Parcae were the three Fates of Ancient Rome: Nona, who spins the thread of life; Decima, who measures out the length of the thread of life; and Morta, the third Parcae, who cuts the thread of life.

Page 176:
In situ is Latin for *on site*.

Zeus is the sky and thunder god who rules Mount Olympus.

Euripides (480–406 B.C.) was a playwright of Ancient Greece.

Menandros (Menander) (c. 342/41–290 B.C.) was a Greek dramatist and the best-known representative of Athenian New Comedy

Crescent moons on cupolas refers to the Muslim symbol seen atop mosques.

Medea was, in Greek mythology, an enchantress who helped Jason, leader of the Argonauts, obtain the Golden Fleece from her father, King Aeëtes of Colchis.

Athena was, in Greek mythology, a daughter of Zeus and goddess of wisdom and war.

Attica was an ancient district of east-central Greece; Athens was its chief city.

Page 179:
Helen refers to Helen of Troy. In Greek mythology, this daughter of Zeus was depicted as the cause of the Trojan war.
   Casus belli is an act or event that provokes or is used to justify war.

Page 176:
In the Bible, Abraham's nephew Lot accompanies him from Haran to the land of Canaan (Genesis 12). However, Abraham and Lot eventually separate because the land cannot support both of their possessions, animals, and servants. Abraham allows Lot to pick first the area where he would like to settle.

Page 180:
"Sorrowful City" is excerpted from the novel-in-verse Protokoll, publisheed by Magvetö in 2010.

Page 193:
Thujas are large arborvitae trees.

Page 194:
A corrie is a steep-sided hollow.

Page 196:
A cutty stool is a low stool, often that on which an offender was publicly rebuked during a church service.

Katinka Hosszú (born 3 May 1989) is a Hungarian competitive swimmer who specializes in individual medley events. She is a three-time Olympic champion and a nine-time long-course world champion.

Page 205:

Lake Balaton, the largest freshwater lake in Central Europe, is located about fifty miles southwest of Budapest.

Page 212:
Fata Morgana is a kind of mirage by which distant objects appear inverted, distorted, displaced, or multiplied.